Life Long Learning ~ Transforming Learning

Discovering Learning Through
Living Life in Unlimitless Possibility

Dr. Patti Diamondlady Diamond, DD

~

For further details about Life Long Learning, visit our website at

http://www.lifelonglearning4all.com

~

ISBN: 1-4116-2492-0

Printed in the United States of America

First Edition

10 9 8 7 6 5 4 3 2 1

Table of Contents

Do not train children into learning by force and harshness, but direct them to it by what amuses their minds ~ Plato

Acknowledgements

To my wonderful husband, Aaron, without your love, strength, complete trust, faith, and support, I would be free from ever making it through. I love you!

~

To our beautiful children ~ Chris, Matthew, and Anthony, this book is for you, Without you there would be no book, You are my sunshine, You have shown me more about life and learning than I have ever been able to show you, You are the most precious gifts to this world. I love you!

~

To my dad and mom, you are the wind beneath my wings, my catalysts to learning in life and such wonderful gifts to me and to the world

~

To Tracy, dearest friend, without you this book would be free from ever being published, words will ever be free from expressing the gratitude I feel for your gifts of love. Thank you from the depths of my heart and soul

~

For no matter where knowledge, learning, and wisdom come from ~ no matter what shape, size, or dimension it assumes ~ it is still what it is ~ knowledge, learning, and wisdom. Therefore, they should always be embraced. That knowledge, learning, and wisdom when utilized, when placed into action, illuminates a shining light forth like that of a lighthouse beacon for all to encompass. This vision is priceless and provides an opening for others to follow in what is being modeled ~ Unknown

Introduction

Life Long Learning......Such a simple concept, and yet, by the same token, such a complex one. Our journey toward Life Long Learning has been an amazing one. And yet, we are still very much on this path, as we will remain on it for the rest of our lives. It was a remarkable set of circumstances that thrusted us toward this incredible journey. It is that journey and all we have learned from it thus far, that is what I wish to share with you within the pages of this book.

As with any journey one takes in this lifetime, it has not always been an easy one. The struggle to move from institutional learning to Life Long Learning was at times a lengthy, arduous process[Compulsory education] damaged my children's sense of self-esteem and self worth. As a teacher in both the private and public school arena, I saw countless children suffering at the hands of a system that cannot possibly fulfill each child's own individual needs, all the while knowing that there must be another way.

Through it all, once we began to see the light at the end of the tunnel ⚡learning freedom, for all of us, it has been a path of discovery that has truly been worth everything we have been through. There behind the clouds, is now this beautiful rainbow of light cascading down upon us and upon our lives. After many, many years of research and soul searching, I believe that I have found that other way through the concept of Life Long Learning. This is the gift of a labor of love that I wish to give to you now.

It is my dearest and fondest wish within the pages of this book to be able to bestow the gift to you that took me quite a long period of time to accumulate ~ valuable research, insight, and wisdom. This research, these insights, and this wisdom have enabled me to develop the confidence and the serenity in knowing that Life Long Learning really ***is*** the most amazing present you can give to yourself and your children. I know in my heart, without a doubt, that Life Long Learning is the most precious offering I could have ever given to my children. Not only to them, but something truly amazing began to happen as this present began to unfold in our lives.

We all know the saying of "What you place out into the world comes back to you tenfold". I truly believe in this saying, because I have always believed that what you put out in life, be it positive or negative energy, comes back to you and sometimes yes, even ten fold. This is exactly what began to transpire as Life Long Learning came to be for us.

The learning, the serenity, the awe-inspiring wonder ~ all that and more came back to me ten fold! I have too, been given this gift back in a very special way from my children to me. They have shown me so much of the world through their eyes and have opened my eyes to so many concepts, such wisdom, and knowledge, that I would have never *dreamed* of learning had it not been for them showing me the way.

I then began to see with my own two eyes that Life Long Learning is contagious. The joy of freedom in learning through life began to trickle down to my husband, to my parents, my brother, my sister-in-law, my husband's family, my friends. It seems everywhere I look around now, the idea of unlimitless possibilities in learning outside of what conventional "school" tells us we *have to,* seems to appeal on so many levels, to so many people. I knew at that moment what I was being called to do in life. This then became the true inspiration for this book ~ that Life Long Learning can be for all. Not just for our children, but for us, all of us on this earth!

Life Long Learning is not about a destination to get to or how to "teach" your child "subjects" like reading and math or "teaching" them what they need to know for life. Life Long Learning is just what it says it is…a way of being, a way of life, learning your whole life long, learning and growing together as a family through life. As we are all connected, therefore, we are all one family.

My vision within the pages of this book is to illustrate to you a unique way of life and of learning. A way that I believe within time, will come to be more like the norm and not so "unique." The learning within each individual will always remain unique, as each person is unique. However, the way in which we learn, I believe will transcend with each person whom embraces Life Long Learning. I hope that this book will be the catalyst for this transformation to come to fruition.

It is not to say that this way is the only or the best way to learn. It is merely what works for us and for those around us. I hope that within the pages of this book that you will take what it is that you embrace and utilize it to its fullest capability, whatever it is that resonates with you and whatever does not resonate with you discard. The choice will be yours. My dream is that you will come to embrace Life Long Learning as our family has, for the freedom that is available for you and you family. I hope that this too becomes your dream, so that together, we can transform learning, one person, and one family at a time.

Please come and enjoy the journey with me. Allow me to give this gift to you now. Allow me not to "teach" you anything, but rather to show you the path. So that then you too, will begin your own Life Long Learning journey and forward the learning on to others ~

Cool Runnings ~ Peace Be the Journey!

Infinite Love, Light, and Blessings to You Always,
Dr. Patti Diamondlady Diamond, DD

Knowledge is not enough, unless it leads you to understanding, and, in turn, to wisdom.

~ Sarnoff, "Youth in a Changing World," 1954

Chapter One

What Life Long Learning is...
and What it is Not

Many people have asked me this puzzling question...... "Just what *is* Life Long Learning?" Many people think that they know Life Long Learning by its more widely recognized name – Unschooling. To me, though, the simple word "unschooling" seems to represent "anti" learning, as if to be an act of defiance to learning. Learning is quite the contrary actually, and so is Life Long Learning.

While unschooling tends to lend itself to providing children with a nontraditional, noncompulsory "schooling" environment or the simple act of not "doing school at home", I believe this concept that John Holt pioneered, the essence of what is termed Unschooling, is really Life Long Learning. This reference to learning therefore, should be given a name that promotes a sense of freedom, serenity, and contentment. There is nothing "anti" in the words Life Long Learning. In fact, Life Long Learning opens the door to the endless possibilities that life has to offer for learning and much more, which is what we all want for our children, for ourselves, is it not?

Life Long Learning is much more than just a concept pioneered by a man forty or so years ago though. It is a taking of his initial vision and expanding upon it to include much more. Life Long Learning, in its simplest of terms is learning that is individual led, interest driven, natural, and self-directed. It is creative, it is spontaneous, and it is remarkable...very much unlike the structure of institutional learning. So, what does *that* mean, you might ask? In the context of our children's learning in life it means allowing your child the time, freedom, and space to learn what, when, how and where *they* choose to. It is a trusting of and in your child that he/she will learn what they need to learn, when they need to learn it, and how they need to learn it ~ without having their learning dictated to them through curricular mandate to be done at a specific time and place.

Think back to the time when your child was first born.....Did he/she have to be "taught" how to cry, how to wet a diaper, or how to breast/formula feed? No, rather than being "taught", they simply learned on their own how to do these things. They may have needed to be "guided" to the breast/bottle initially, but the rest was done solely on their own. When it came time for your child to crawl, stand, walk, and talk....did they need to be "taught" this? Again, strikingly, the answer to this question is No. They may have needed your guidance ~ an environment rich with opportunity, encouragement, and love, which enabled them to learn and do these things, however, there was no formalized "teaching" involved in it. None of us, as parents, propped our child up on the couch and said "Ok, TALK". Nor did we forcibly maneuver our child's legs into a walking motion. All we did was simply provide the environment necessary and then trusted in our children to learn what they needed to learn. The Life Long Learning concept, therefore, works this same way.

As humans, we are created with an innate sense of learning, a natural curiosity about the world around us and all that is within that world. It is instinctive. It is as innate to us as breathing. It need not be cajoled, or bribed, or forced in any way. To do so only stifles that learning and that love of learning. Meaningful knowledge and wisdom can only occur when a child *wants* to learn. The desire to learn must come from within. We all were born with this innate desire.

 It is only when we are "forced" into learning within a "school" environment, that this innate sense of learning ultimately over time, is quelled. This why children struggle so and do so poorly within an institutional learning environment as they are "forced" to learn and to "perform". They are forced to acquire knowledge of certain number of "facts" that have no meaning to them or to their lives, within a certain period of time. Children are then "required to perform" such facts in a repetitious manner in the way of tests and rote memorizations ~ commonly known as "school work", "seat work", "assignments", or "homework" ~ rather than being given the time, opportunity, and space to accumulate knowledge on their own and in their own way.

One does not need a "test" or "rote memorization schoolwork and homework" to know that they have learned something and that they "know" it. Once you have learned something, whatever it is, you have learned it. If, as you were "taught" in school, you are made to just "memorize" it, spit it out on a test, then forget it, it has not been truly learned, not even once, yet.

Just as when you first learned how to ride a bicycle. After many years of not implementing this action, it may take you a while to remember how, but you already acquired the knowledge of how at some point in your life, therefore, you do not need to be taught how to ride a bicycle again. You merely need to recall it from your memory to accomplish the task at hand. Therefore, learning stays with you permanently, it does not go away on a whim.

Observations Within the "Institutional Learning Environment" ~ The Cost to Children

Have you ever been on a field trip to a museum with a school? Or have you ever been to a museum or a place where there are "schooled" children on a field trip? Have you ever watched the expressions on the children's faces and the expressions in their bodies? Even more interesting still, is to observe how children are treated and how they express themselves within the "schooled environment".

I spent many years as both a teacher working in both public/private schooling sector and as a parent volunteer observing this phenomenon. From all of those years of observation several things became all to clear to me. Children begin their "schooling" endeavor with their minds free and full of a love of learning. They are like sponges with a willingness and readiness to absorb anything about life that they can. At first, when forced to learn what the teacher or school says they must learn, the child attempts to accomplish just that. They do so because, at this point, they love to learn and are eager to please their teachers and parents. The forced learning is in the disguise of fun, games, and activities that the children enjoy.

However, what seems to happen with this forced learning over time is that the learning takes on a more demanding form. The children become increasingly aware that the "fun and games" turns into drill and practice, and drill and practice some more. This drill and practice then becomes the child's way of life. Therefore, children are not only being told what to learn, but how, where, and when to learn. They are in essence being instructed, subtly, without ever being told that this is indeed what is transpiring, that they are incapable of learning unless a teacher teaches them.

Children are also "taught" within the institutional setting that life, just as in school, must be divided into subjects ~ Math, Reading, Science, History, etc. And that learning must be "done" within a certain time frame. Children are made to feel that unless they continue the drill and practice; that unless they "perform" at a certain level, that they are not competent to move onto the next level of learning. Children are also led to believe that there is only one way to learn ~ the way the teacher says you should learn and you should never question that way of learning or the teacher. To do deviate from that learning that has been taught or to question the teacher's authority in any way, will only serve to place you under punishment in the form of a reprimand or "poor grade".

Children are also "taught" segregation by age in the schooling environment. As an example, children are told that they may only play with "2nd graders" if they are a second grader on the playground, and anyone who comes into the "2nd grade" play area is immediately reprimanded. Thus, segregation by other means tends to ensue within the "age groups". This happens in the form of "cliques" or groups of children who are only liked if they are or act a "certain way". These children must have the right hairstyle or the right clothes or have money or be popular in order to be liked. If this is not the case, then they are ostracized, teased, and ridiculed for being the unique individual that they are. The children whom do not fit in are also given labels for being who they are, such as "geek" or "ugly" or "fat".

Socializing is something that is taught to children as prohibited while in the schooling endeavor. Evidence of this is seen in the following statements that are uttered over and over again by teachers and school staff ~ "Be quiet in class and do your work" and "You may not talk to your friends during class time, this is not a social hour". The oxymoron of this is that we are made to believe that one of the reasons we are to send our children to school are so that they may be properly "socialized".

What tends to happen then is by the time a child reaches about the age of 9 to 10 is that children will either attempt to rebel against this form of degradation or they will be quieted into submission. This is about the time that we start seeing the "bad report cards", the "notes home from the teacher" or the punitive punishments such as, detention, or having to stay in at recess and lunch.

Or we may see what is termed as the "quiet good child", a child who has become quiet and withdrawn but for the most part to outward appearances "seems" to be doing fine in school. For some children, they will continue to spend the rest of their "schooling" career trying to break out of this mold, as if in a cry for help. For some, they will in essence continue to be "quieted" into submission with constant disciplinary penalties if they should deviate from what is considered to be "improper behavior". Both avenues leave children feeling helpless and powerless in their world. Both avenues only serve to make life outside of institutional learning an unbearable one.

Thus, over time child soon grows to hate learning. The love of learning and the bright learning in their eyes, that once was there, turns into a child who is cold, distant and dislikes anything that even resembles learning. Worse still, is the loss of self worth and confidence by being made to feel "less than" for not "performing" to expectation.

Back to the Beginning Then...

Let us go back now, to the questions that I asked at the beginning of observations section, which was this... Have you ever been on a field trip to a museum with a school? Or have you ever been to a museum or a place where there are "schooled" children on a field trip? Have you ever watched the expressions on the children's faces and the expressions in their bodies?

If you ever have been in the presence of a group of children on a field trip, you will notice that their love of learning, their awe of the world is drained right out of their faces. You have the majority of the class just walking around aimlessly with the teacher and the tour guide. You can observe tell from the expressions on their faces and in their body language that they do not want to be there. One could almost read their minds to hear the children say statements like ~ "This is **so** boring", "I wish my mom/dad were here", "I wish could go play and explore the museum place myself", or "Why do we have to look at **this** exhibit now, I would find this other one over here more interesting now, "I wish I could go see this interesting thing over there, instead of having to just "follow" the group".

Most children therefore, are in a place they do not choose to be in, with individuals they do not necessarily wish to be with, and not able to explore and learn in a manner in which they want to or to take the time longer at one place to explore than another. An example of this could be that maybe they are not interested in dinosaurs, but they do like rocks and crystals. However, in a schooling environment, "the group is moving right along"; therefore, that child cannot stay to absorb the enjoyment of the rocks and crystals.

Life After the "Schooling" Experience

Under the current conditions in which we as a societal whole, force children to learn in an institutional setting, that environment takes on the look and feel of a negative experience for children. If you are to take a look at the surroundings of a school, you will find that it is set up very much like a prison. Not only the surroundings, but the overall atmosphere of a school is conducive to that of a prison–like feel. Our children (that of my husband Aaron and me) own children came up with this analogy of their own volition. They could see how the fences that are erected in an attempt to keep children safe really make them feel like they are prisoners. Also too, our children surmised, that being that children do not have the freedom to leave at any given time and that the learning becomes stagnant or not geared to what their interests are, this too lends itself to a prison-like atmosphere.

Conversely, if a child is given the opportunity to choose their form of learning and is then there within the schooling environment by choice, then school therefore is not all of those afore mentioned things. In other words, school can only be a positive learning environment *if* children are allowed to learn freely what they want when they want to, without learning being forced. Therefore, if a child chooses to go to school and they are not forced to go by societal, parental, or family influences, and the child can be free to leave when the learning is not of their interest and come back when it is, then the schooling environment can be a positive experience.

Unfortunately, for most children today, however, school is not of choice, it is of by demand. It is by the force of societal pressures to conform, that we attempt to make our children comply with what is told that they *have* to learn. If most children were given the choice to be apart of or not be apart of the institutional setting, most would choose not to be. Most would choose to learn in a modality that is of their own choosing. Therefore, if we allow our children to choose school as their form of learning and they choose not to, then why should we force them to attend school? If we are truly to give children back their own personal power, then why force learning? Simply because children are smaller and we feel somehow that they would appear to be more helpless than us as adults? Does this make their choices any less valid than ours?

I believe that size, nor age, should not be a factor in the path of life we choose, which includes that of learning. In fact, we all have since birth instinctively made choices in our lives without ever giving much consideration to the fact that this was indeed what we were doing. As infants even, we chose to crawl, here or there. We choose to eat when we are hungry. As an infant, our way of choosing would be to cry to let our mother know we were hungry. As toddlers, we chose to walk here or there. And so the process continues throughout life, thereby showing that as humans, we are indeed capable of making choices. There may be times in one's life where we may need direction and focus in order to make our choices in life, but whether it is deemed by the rest of the world as good or bad, right or wrong, we all have the capacity to make our own choices in life.

 The lack of choice within compulsory education then brings to mind, what does life look like for these children, now adults, after being subjected to the inability to choose for themselves for twelve plus years within the institutional setting? What has happened is we have all of these adults who go out into what is termed by society as the "real world", as if we have not been in the real world all these years. In fact, we have not been in the "real world" all of these years. Using the previously mentioned analogy, we can see how we have been "locked away" as it were within the "schooling environment" being told how, what, when, and where to learn, obtain friendships, live, and the like.

Thus, upon entering the "real world", we are hit with a *major* culture shock when embarking into the world as an adult outside of the "schooled" environment. Much like that of a prisoner, whom has just been released back into mainstream society after a prolonged stay in prison, many are hit with a dose of *big time* culture shock, due to the fact they soon discover that life is *not* divided into subjects, as they had been "taught" for all of those years. They soon start to feel even more helpless because they do not feel that they can learn anything on their own, without being "taught" how.

As adults then, we wander helplessly through society, trying to "make it" in the world, without any *real* life skills to conjure a worthwhile life for ourselves and our future generation. We are left with that age old question they ask you from the time you are little…."What do you want to be when you grow up?" For most of us, we just settle for what we can make out of life ~ we get a "job", we fall in love, get married, and have families of our own. For most of us, we just live out our lives never realizing the full potential of our possibilities for life.

Now, for some, we are happy with that. We are content with just living our lives until we die with what we have and how we have come to exist in this world and do not question what more there is. But there are some of us, myself included, who have always seen a vision ~ who have always known that there is something out there that is better than just living our lives this way. For us, we know that there is an endless stream of possibilities of what life is and can be. We long to bring this infinite source of possibilities into our lives, the lives of our children and of their children's children. ***This***, is where Life Long Learning begins!

What Life Long Learning Looks Like

With Life Long Learning, there is no end. It is a continuous circle of learning and connections to learning, as there is no "timetable" to learning. For those of us for whom compulsory education was a way of life and we knew no better, did we at the end of our "schooling", then all of the sudden because we completed high school or college, stop learning? No! We did not say to ourselves, "Ok, I have "graduated" now; I think I will stop learning!" The truth is that we learn our whole lives, not just when we were "in school", because life in of itself *is* a learning process. We will continue to learn until we take our very last breath. Even death is a learning process.

A friend of mine, who was considering Life Long Learning, stated to me that she was afraid to start Life Long Learning at that point in her daughter's life. She made the statement that she thought it too late to be "messing around with her learning". My response to her was the following.....

"Why is it too late to be messing around with her learning? Too late for what? Your daughter's life has only just begun! So, she is a teenager, and? If you figure that the average life expectancy of a human being is approximately 80 years of age, I think, that leaves her ALOT of learning and growing ahead of her! She has her whole life ahead of her to view and experience the world around her!"

None of us, child or adult alike, learn exactly the same way. There is no such thing as only one or just a few types of "learning styles" for everyone, as compulsory education has lead us to believe. Much debate and "categorizing" of learning into styles and subjects has surfaced over the years. However, the fact remains that multiple learning styles within one person is inherently possible and is what makes each person an individual, is what makes each person unique. Therefore ~ how, when, and in what time frame our learning is to occur ~ should be as individual and unique as we are and should be left only up to us.

Remember, as I spoke of before, that in school, we are taught that individuals **need** to learn in "subjects" ~ Reading, Writing, Math, Science, and History etc. ~ that these "subjects" need to be taught in a certain order and within a certain time frame. Also, compulsory education has taught us that you **must** learn one set of concepts first before going onto the next set of concepts. The truth is though; life is not divided into subjects. Nor do we necessarily need to learn adding of 2 or 3 digits **before** being able to learn multiplication. As an example, it is just as logical to see that a child can go from learning basic addition facts, to learning multiplication in the natural progression of life. When you learn that 2 + 2 = 4, it is then quite easy to make the leap to seeing that 2 x 2 =4 because there are two sets of two. Therefore, one does not **have to** learn one first before the other, despite what we are told we **have** to in school.

What Do I Need to "Do"?

One of the main objectives of Life Long Learning is that of choice. As noted earlier, freedom of a child to choose what, when, how and where he/she wishes to learn is one of the most beautiful and awe-inspiring gifts that a parent can ever give to a child, or to themselves for that matter. It really does not require you to "**do**" anything, as you do not "**do**" Life Long Learning. Life Long Learning is just what it says it is…. learning your whole life long – living, learning, and growing together.

One of the many advantages of this is that you, the parent, are not required to become someone else, i.e. a professional teacher pouring knowledge at and into child-vessels on a planned basis. You do not need to provide "curriculum" or make your child sit down and do worksheets and tests. Should your child want to or choose to do these things, than they may, but it is not compulsory.

Instead, you live and learn **with your child**, together, pursuing questions and interests as they arise. "Leading by example", as the old adage goes, is an **extremely powerful** way to provide a rich Life Long Learning environment. This adage is often used to imply that parents must show a good or proper example of behavior in order for children to follow, however, this same adage can also apply to learning throughout life. If you as a parent develop an active interest in learning in the world, in viewing things from a new perspective, in a new light, modeling this then will bring about what I call "contagious learning".

It is then the utilizing of a "world of unlimitless possibilities for learning" ~ along with, yours and their own passions/interests, which is what gives birth to Life Long Learning. It is the shifting of perspectives, from textbooks to the real world that we learn best. Choosing to build a Lego village will invite the opportunity to learn much about math, geometry, culture, maybe even history depending on the type of village. Therefore, the variety of "subjects" that compulsory education wishes to instill upon children can be easily learned in a non-subject like manner, but rather in an open learning manner in the way the child chooses.

Children grow to hate the very "subjects" that are taught in school simply because they are not given the opportunity to "experience" them. History, for example, is often dislike so strongly mainly because a child is told "Sit, read these chapters, answer these questions, and when you are finished, there will be a test next week to see if you "learned" it or not" ~ rather than being given the opportunity to experience what I call "Living History", History in a hands-on manner.

A wonderful example of "Living History" is when a friend of mine took her four children on a trip along the Oregon Trail from start to finish. Her children actually experienced first hand, what life was like during the 1840's to 1850's and can easily share with anyone all that they learned from their journey. My own children have experienced the westward movement of the pioneers, while visiting Pioneer Arizona.

You do not need to "know everything'" in order to provide a Life Long Learning environment for your children or your family. Sometimes, all your children will want and/or need is conversation with you. My children and I will sit and talk for **hours** about anything that interests them, and often times one conversation about one thing, will lead into another conversation completely about something else. Sometimes, I will know the information they are seeking, and they will listen intently to my vast knowledge and wisdom. Other times, I do not have any idea what the answer is. My job, as their parent, then is to provide them with the resources and a way to find those resources. Children, given the freedom to do so and by their very own innate nature, when not knowing the answer to a certain question or a particular interest they have that they do not have the knowledge on, become quite capable of seeking out a person to assist them in finding the answers they seek. That person the majority of the time will be you, their parent, but, this is not always the case.

The information and knowledge that our children seek, need not be expensive to obtain either. We live in an 'information-rich' society, and there is a vast amount of information to buy, to seek, to view, or to obtain for free ~ libraries, television, museums and historic buildings are available to all ~ all you need is to investigate what is around you and seize every opportunity to collect 'information ' on whatever interests your child. In every local community there will be enthusiasts in many hobbies or professions who are usually more than willing to share their expertise; sometimes friends or neighbors may happily offer special knowledge and resources as well.

In these next chapters, I will bring to life examples to show to you Life Long Learning in action. Life Long Learning in action is to do simply just, what the words say and mean – Live you Life and Learn all day, everyday. Life Long Learning provides the concepts and practical use on a daily basis of ever-important skills such as ~ how to learn, how to think, how to find information, and where to look. Your whole family then is likely to become more resourceful, use more initiative; often you will learn alongside each other, enjoying each other's curiosity and the thrill of discovery.

~

"Children grow up believing that life is like school, with every question having an answer in the back of the book. Maturity consists in recognizing that life is a continuing series of multiple choice questions with the answers torn out of the back of the book."
~ Sydney Harris

If learning is such a good thing, why do you think you have to force it on me? ~ Donald, age six

Chapter Two

Deschooling, Immersion of Learning, Inclusivity of Learning ~ The Three Phases of Life Long Learning

Within the Life Long Learning process, there are three main phases. Generally, one phase will blend seamlessly into the next. At times one will intertwine with another. It may be a long process or a shorter one. This varies greatly from one individual or one family to the next. Conversely, for those children whom have never had to set foot inside of a school, the first phase, that of *Deschooling*, is one of which they will, happily so, not need to partake in. These children will for all intents and purposes, be able to with ease, flow right into phase two~ *Immersion of Learning* and phase three ~ *Inclusivity of Learning*.

However, for those children who are currently within or whom have just recently left the institutional learning environment, and adults who were as children in this setting, it may prove to be a daunting task if one does not know the process in which a child and parent need to go through in order to fully encompass Life Long Learning in it's entirety. For the purposes of this book then, we will illuminate all three phases for all to know.

Phase One ~ Deschooling

The first phase in the Life Long Learning process is deschooling. The first question that comes to mind is ~ do children need deschooling time upon leaving compulsory education? Oh yes, very much so. It is quite important to free ourselves from the constraints that are placed upon us when it the compulsory educational environment. I like to think of it as like a shedding of skin, the way a snake does. We need to shed the skin of the schooling experience, getting rid of the old, to make way for the new. Deschooling specifically refers to a period of adjustment experienced by children removed from school settings. Simply put, it is taking the time to let go of the notion that "school" is the only and best way of doing and of learning. It also includes the ability of parents to deschool themselves ~ that is, the unlearning of concepts and beliefs about the nature and purpose of learning. School-based methods of instruction and thinking, such as the demanding of "work" being done in the form of worksheets, tests, and repetitive tasks, rarely translate directly into Life Long Learning. The reason is such that when these methods are tried, often parents run into the same kinds of problems faced by teachers in schools!

Children and parents who have been in a traditional school setting often have to take another approach to Life Long Learning initially. Traditional schooling can cause the loss of intrinsic motivation and the pure joy of learning. The process of recovering those gifts is usually what is called "deschooling." It is the process of healing, learning to know oneself, and escaping the expectations and forms of traditional schools.

But...My Children Are Not Doing Anything!

In an 1998 interview with Emily Subler, Sandra Dodd, a former *Home Education Magazine* columnist, says it best about deschooling, when in this interview she states~

"We have voices and ghosts inside us, and conditioning, all of which keep us from homelearning clearly, joyfully, and calmly. We have guilt and fear and "ideas" [bad ideas] tied up with our thoughts of learning/education, and it just gums up our brains and our hearts. People think learning has to happen on a schedule, and incrementally, and they get that idea from "courses" of study, school years, semesters, and graded textbooks. People fear that if teachers go to school for years to become teachers that they must know something and that this arcane knowledge is the key to learning. People fear that without "A Permanent Record", their child will grow up without an identity, without a reality, and might never get married or reproduce. School phrases like "being a student is a full-time job" and "what you do here will affect your entire life" and "you have to learn to get along with people, so no, we're not going to transfer you to a teacher you can stand" live in the heads of people who went to school for twelve to eighteen years, and if we didn't

question them then, are we safe to question them now, with our tender children's futures in the balance?" She goes on to say, "Deschooling means dismantling the overlay of school. Gradually (or just all of a sudden, if you have that ability) stop speaking and thinking in terms of grades, semesters, schooldays, education, scores, tests, introductions, reviews, and performance, and replace those artificial structures and measures with ideas like morning, hungry, happy, new, learning, interesting, playing, exploring and living."

In the beginning, it may very well seem like our children are not "doing" anything. In a sense, we are correct. As children, as well as, ourselves, need to have to do just as Sandra Dodd spoke of. It is a form of "deprogramming" if you will of all of the artificial means of learning that has been so ingrained into us. We need to stop thinking, feeling, and breathing school, and begin to learn again how to trust our own innate learning abilities just like we once did when we were younger and had no concept that "school" even existed.

Amount of Time Deschooling Takes ~
What Does Deschooling Look Like?

The practical aspects of deschooling are simply time, space, and freedom. Within this time, both children and parents need to rid themselves of all "school" thoughts. This includes classes, teaching, instruction, textbooks, worksheets, tests, and school phrases. We need to distinguish the difference between "teach" and "learn". Also, during this time we must come to accept that grades, diplomas, curriculum, and exterior motivations, (i.e. rewards, stickers, candies and the like) should not define who we are in terms of the how and why we learn or want to learn. It is the realizing that the whole world is related and interrelated; that life and learning are not divided into subjects.

It is a time to examine what our passions are and what it is that we wish to learn. It is a knowing that we can and will learn what we wish to, when we are ready to. Deschooling gives us "permission" to eliminate coercion of learning and to appreciate that what is important to us to learn, grows and transforms as we grow and transform. It is a realizing that no matter where knowledge, wisdom, and learning come from ~ no matter what form, shape, size, or dimension it assumes ~ it is still what it is, knowledge, wisdom, and learning. Therefore knowledge, wisdom, and learning should always be embraced. It is about the freedom to explore and change our passions. It is an understanding that learning is as constant as the flow of the ocean tide. Deschooling becomes that period of intense questioning and of challenging yourself to think differently, to think outside of the "box", and beyond our comfort zone. This, at times, may seem like it is difficult to accomplish, however, it can be done. It can be done with a belief that it can be done, as our beliefs shape our realities. Just as with all learning, this will only occur when we are ready and willing to.

It has been suggested that it takes one year of deschooling for every year you spend in school. This will vary with each individual, each child. Just as in learning, we all will take however long or short we may need to deschool. For myself, I believe it has taken most of the fourteen plus years that I was in school to equally deschool. Being a former teacher in the private and public school systems, seeing first hand what my role was in perpetuating this stifling environment was and its' effects and as a volunteer, observing my own children's suffering at the hands of the system, only helped to accelerate the deschooling process for me. I know that for our children, the process has been as unique as each of the three of them are. Chris, our oldest, whom spent the most amount of time within the schooling environment, one would think, would need the most amount of time to deschool. However, this is not the case. In fact, he deschooled quite rapidly. My rationalization for this, beyond the fact that each child's deschooling is unique, is the mere fact that he, much like myself, has always had an "out of the box" approach to life. He is a young man wise beyond his years and has the capability to grasp concepts that even I at times grapple with.

Now, in contrast, our middle son Matthew, whom had been in the school setting for two and one half years, for him deschooling was a concept that was harder for him to grasp. For him, the ingrained form of "socializing" (which I discuss in further detail in chapter eleven) was more a part of schooling for him than anything that they attempted to teach him. That and the fact that because he had been told for those years that he could not learn for himself, he doubted himself so very much that he could learn, almost to the point of a very low self esteem and poor self image. Matthew, then upon leaving school, struggled for a time with the concept of "I will miss my friends, whom can I play with?" concept, not realizing that he never really had a bond with any of these children other than within school. He never once saw these children outside of the schooling environment, as he had nothing in commonality with any of these children outside of school.

Matthew did have two friends, both of which no longer even went to the same school as he did when he left, that we still keep in contact with, as they share interests outside of school and always had. He also struggled with the concept that he could learn on his own ~ how, when, where, and what he wish to learn when he wished to learn it. This was a concept that was quite foreign to him, and took quite a while for him to come into on his own. Aside from those two friends he kept in touch with still, it did take quite a while for Matthew to realize that friends can be made of all ages, not just those of "his age group" and that there are opportunities all around us to make friends, that making and having relationships does not only come from school, that one can create and maintain friendships outside of the institutional learning environment.

The Guitar

I can remember once during our deschooling processing of how much of a lesson of learning it was for me when Matthew had developed an interest in the guitar. I thought I was doing the "good mom" thing and "purchased" a video for him, a "how to be taught guitar" type video along with the guitar. Based upon his reaction to it, you would have thought it was the end of the world! What I realized was by purchasing that video without him coming to me first and asking for it was that I was controlling his learning and telling him in essence that I did not feel that he was smart enough to learn it on his own that he must need to be taught.

This was *very* much the "schooling" in me coming out, because it has been ingrained into me from day one in "school" that if you do not know something, that you must be too stupid enough to learn and figure it out on your own, and that you need a "teacher" or some other form of instruction to be able to learn anything in life. Matthew showed me that this is so not the case. I learned that day too, that children will learn what they need to learn from a particular thing that interest them *how* they need to and *if* they are not sure, then that child will come to you and ask you how, without you having to "impose" your way of thinking or learning on them. So, while he did not want to take lessons, he did want to learn how to play it "on his own" as he said to me that day, very much a Life Long Learning way of thinking and being. So when this occurs, rather than "teaching him", I just encouraged him in anyway I can and provide him with the resources if and when he asks for them.

During his deschooling process, ***anything*** having to do with lessons or teachers or "being taught" anything, Matthew would immediately freak out, which was the deschooling process in him! In fact in many ways today he still feels this way. After all he was put through in "school" is it any wonder really? The deschooling process, just like that of Life Long Learning has much to do about trust ~ trusting in your child, and trusting that your child is capable of knowing and learning, and however that may happen is truly up to them.

Allowing Matthew ~ just as allowing any child in the deschooling process of Life Long Learning ~ the freedom, time, and space to discover this theory for himself, at times proved to be a daunting task. There were times when I felt uneasy and unsure that he would ever be able to understand the concept of learning on his own again the way he did when he was younger and feel comfortable in his own skin enough to branch out to do so. We spent many, many hours together talking about it. It also took him observing the fact that myself and others around him had developed friendships outside of a "schooled" situation and were learning without the coercion of school. Eventually, he was able to move through the aspect of deschooling, but it did take him a lot long than Chris. It took him time to begin to trust himself again. Had my husband and I not given him the freedom, time, and space to do so, I do not think he would have walked away with the sense of self confidence and pride in himself that he has now.

With our youngest son, Anthony, deschooling did not have much value to him really. Being that he had only spent a little more than a year in school, and had only one what I would perceive as a really "negative" experience and several minor ones, so deschooling to him came rather quick and effortlessly. This in no way trivializes what happened to him while in school. It, in and of itself was quite traumatic to him and started to turn that love of learning into one of contempt. I feel quite blessed to have been able to allow him to deschool when I did. He is all the happier for me having done so.

Anthony is a child who is as they say "ahead of is time". At the age of four, I had requested that he be placed in Pre-Kindergarten, as the teacher in me could see that he was very advanced for his age within "schooling standards". Thus, at the age of four and a half, he began Kindergarten. All was fine for him until after "graduating" private school Kindergarten, we placed him in public school. Public school informed us that he would have to "repeat" Kindergarten, regardless of how intelligent and advanced he was, simply because he was not "age appropriate" for first grade. His birthday is in January, and the "cutoff" for the "appropriate" grade is in December, so in the school's eyes he would not "qualify".

This upset Anthony greatly, and caused him much distress. He would ask me things like, "What is wrong with me mommy? Why will they not let me learn? All I want to do is just be in first grade and learn. The stuff they are teaching me back in Kindergarten I know already and it is boring". My heart broke when hearing him utter these words. I pushed the school at that point to move him to first grade, and they told me he had to have "assessments" done first, before they would even consider it. I watched for three weeks, as day after day, Anthony would come home upset, frustrated, and sad, all because he had to do these "tests" in order to "make the grade". It was then that I knew all of the research I had done on Life Long Learning, that it was time to make the move and pull our boys out of that environment. Anthony did go to a private first grade for a few short months, in an attempt to give private school a try, only to have the same situation occur for him there as it did in public school. Thus, at that point, I knew it was time. Therefore, Anthony's deschooling did not take as long, as though he had a hard time, it was for such a short time that deschooling for him was a breeze, something of which he enjoyed!

During the deschooling time, it is best if parents do not focus to much on what or whether your child is learning. In truth, even in deschooling process, there is much that our children learn. Parents often believe that if a child is merely "just playing", "just doing a video game", or "just playing on the computer", that they are not learning. In fact, children learn much from "just playing". Just as they did when they were much younger, children learn much about the world and how to figure out the world around them through play. It often helps to view children's "doing nothing" in "educational" terms. In the beginning of the deschooling process, this gives us a way in which to better relate to the fact that they are learning. It is sometimes "seeing" beyond what we feel as "nothing" to know that it is learning.

An example that seeing beyond to know that learning can still occur without "school" while deschooling, comes from when our children first went to the Science Museum just after we began deschooling. When we went in, the boys went "through" the museum what I call the "school" mentality. They ran around to each exhibit like a bunch of crazed lunatics not really taking the time to observe or thoroughly enjoy the hands on interactive science that was available to them. Not to mention that they would not even *consider* going to the Natural History museum, as they all three told me "Oh *that* is boring, we don't want to go *there*!"

However, in contrast, just one month into our deschooling process we went back again. This time, they could not *wait* to go. To my shock and surprise, they actually **wanted** to go. Then, when they were there, we spent almost 3 hours there. They took the time to actually do the experiments and see how things work. It was amazing to see the relaxed expressions in their bodies and that they were "learning" without being forced to. That day, we even went to the Natural History museum! We saw a Feathered Dinosaurs and spent another two hours there exploring, **really** learning and exploring together, with wonder and awe in their eyes and excitedness for learning in their bodies and in their minds. This visit to the natural history museum that day also spurred on Matthew's interest in dinosaurs again, with Matthew wanting to and asking me if he could research with me on the internet more information on the feathered dinosaurs.

The following day, at our homelearning parkday group, he proudly showed all of his friends his dinosaur fossil and baby dinosaur egg that he had purchased at the museum the day before. He also enthusiastically told everyone "I learned that just one feathered dinosaurs' wing is the length of my mom's and dad's room! And that two of them put together with its' body would equal forty plus feet wide!" Our children's spirits soared to new levels never realized before that day! Now **that** is Life Long Learning at it's best!

For some parents, when in the deschooling process, will give their child total freedom. I was one of those parents, as I feel that it was the best way for our children to be able to free themselves from the constraints placed upon them while they were in school. I will explain the why and how I did and do this more in-depth in subsequent chapters within this book. Other parents may feel the need to place some, preferably minimal, restrictions on their children's choices. It is important to note, that if a child is given the freedom to choose his or her own activities, they gradually regain their enjoyment of learning just as Matthew did. Sooner or later, they find something that will rekindle the spark, and the damage of that frustrating school experience will then begin to repair itself. I think in the end, once we are out of the schooling experience as adults, that in time, we all finally become deschooled. But it takes years of conscious effort to get rid of the false standards and preconceptions that were drilled into us during the years we spent in institutionalized learning.

I am Bored

Yet another deschooling aspect that can be a challenge for children is that of boredom. Even once the deschooling phase is behind you, there will be at times in Life Long Learning where boredom will attempt to rear it's head. A fellow Life Long Learner once wrote, "It's a valuable lesson to learn to deal with boredom, just like all other emotions." Upon reading that, it occurred to me that she was correct in her observation. Boredom is one of the many emotions that we, as humans, have in life. Just as we learn strategies for how to recognize, distinguish, and be with other emotions, boredom also is one we need to apply these same concepts to.

If a child came and said they was upset over a loss of a friend, would your response be to tell them that they needed to go clean their room? If a child spoke to you saying that they was irritated enough to go punch their brother, would you reply back to them, "Then sit down and draw me a picture"? It would seem to me that this would seem rather inconsiderate and not something that we would likely do to say to a friend in need of some assistance with a problem they are having. I believe that just as we would with a friend, we should help our children when they are at a loss for what to do next and are looking to us for a sense of direction. When children come to us seeking guidance on how to approach any emotional state, we should feel honored for the opportunity to be there for them and give them some coping skills to help them through the process. Sometimes the real message behind "I'm bored" is "I'm feeling lonely and in need of connection with someone and I am not sure what I can do to get over this uncomfortable feeling. What would you do if you were my age, in this moment?"

It is rare that my children will say "I'm bored". Matthew, out of our three boys, is usually the one whom will state that he is, in fact bored. Sometimes the boredom comes in the form of whining or irritability, and other times it will be matter of factly said. Most of the time, I would surmise, that it is an emotional or intellectual connection that he is seeking. It is his way of wanting to connect with me and for me to help him to find something that interests him as he is not sure at that moment what would interest him. Sometimes, it means that he just wants a hug and to sit and talk with me. Having conversations about anything in life, is something he enjoys quite frequently and gives us a chance to bond. Sometimes "bored" means he is tired, low on energy, or that he needs a break from conscious thought. It is in these times that we will put on a video, just snuggle, and "be" together. At times, just "being" with someone ~ no talking, no anything – to just **BE** with someone in that moment in time, is one of the greatest gifts that we can give to another human being.

Other times I would walk with him around the house, suggesting games, toys, art supplies, or musical instruments that he might have forgotten that he had available to him or that he has not seen in a while. I search the house for things that would provide some visual, auditory, or mental stimulation. There are other times too, when it is just simply a matter of a physical need to get out of the house and run around. Across from our house is a park, and we frequently go there to throw a ball or frisbee around, run around with our dogs , or climb on the monkey bars. And sometimes, boredom is a desire to add excitement into their lives. Going for a drive helps. There are times when we just get in the car and *GO!* No real destination in mind, just the excitement of the unknown! If and when we see something that catches our eye, we will stop and explore! The quest in life then is to welcome those opportunities when your child is bored. There will come a time too, when the threshold of your child needing your guidance when bored will transform all on it has own over time. Nurturing, compassion, self-awareness, interpersonal skills, and creativity all come to fruition when the opportunity to turn "I'm bored" becomes an inspirational memory. To expand further on deschooling, I highly suggest a book called *Deschooling Our Lives.* Matt Hern, editor. Gabriola Island, BC: New Society Publishers, 1996, ISBN: 0-865713-42-1.

Phase Two ~ Immersion of Learning

Somewhere around the time that you are enthralled with the deschooling process, you will suddenly find yourself entrenched in the Immersion of Learning phase. Immersion of Learning is really Life Long Learning at its' best. It involves immersing ourselves, and allowing our children to immerse themselves, into the things we feel passionate about learning and doing. This could be anything that is of interest to you or your children. There is no hard and fast rule to this. It need not even be just one passion, but that of many passions. It can also be of just a slight, fleeting interest that you or your children may have at any given time for a few days or weeks. Immersion of learning is just a "being" with learning in life.

Through the parental support of a child and given the time, freedom, and space, a child will often times pursue his/her passions so completely as to develop a career from those passion(s). It is wise that a parent encourage the pursuit of passions, because it may be what the child will ultimately choose to devote his/her life's work to. It is sometimes just as important to know when to take a step back and allow a child the freedom to let go of a passion, when that fervor has completed its cycle for the child.

Many times we are able to do this by simply knowing that there were "connections" made and knowledge learned with this fleeting interest. Observing and developing a real sense of knowing that everything in life is connected and that making those connections is a part of the constant life learning process is crucial. Realizing too, that some things "might" not connect for years, but that may connect in layers of learning over a prolonged period of time, can be one of the most important parts of Immersion of Learning.

Learning and Fun All Rolled Into One!

Learning during this time can become a fun adventure for you and your children! I remember the time when my youngest son, Anthony came into the room wanting to use my paper cutter to cut up his Pokemon cards. Now, at first my husband flipped, not believing for one minute that I should be "allowing" him to cut up his Pokemon card. However, he was not "just cutting up his Pokemon card". He chose a card that was to him "worthless" as he put it; meaning it was of no use to him in within the Pokemon battles. He learned not only how to use a paper cutter but geometric patterning as well, by what we called "slicing and dicing" his card into pieces. He also found out just how hard the card stock used to print Pokemon cards is to cut through tough. He then placed the pieces all together to form his very own puzzle. Not only did he find this to be a ton of fun, but yes, in fact, he was learning! Did I tell him, "Oh Anthony, that's great! You learned geometry etc....?" No. I merely allowed him the opportunity to explore the world before him without being so worried about a few cut up Pokemon cards, and without a label to his learning.

Immersion of Learning can seem at times to be an uncomfortable path to undertake. This is because you are now actually putting Life Long Learning into action: you are surrendering ~ a letting go, if you will and just learning to **BE**. Be in the moment with your child, whatever that moment is for them and for you, at that moment. You will be amazed at all the beauty and wonder you will see in them, in yourself, and in life. It is a matter of being present in the moment with your children that learning can be envisioned. You will be able to embrace this awe-inspiring wonder because you are no longer pushing the three "R's". You are beginning to trust that your child will learn, just as you have spent your whole adult life learning, without the "use" of a "teacher"; without having to be "taught" anything.

You are now Life Long Learning! The more you repeat this process of living and learning together, the easier it will become! Children, just as we adults, really only retain information that we either have a connection to or repeatedly use. Therefore, if you are able to make connections that your child can link to their lives with something you are learning, the more likely they are to retain it for longer than five minutes. As an example, our son Matthew, he loves sea life things. We read a story called, "Commotion in the Ocean" by Giles Andreae and David Wojtowycz, which has in the book his favorite sea life creature, a stingray. The fact it had his favorite sea life creature, and the fact that we took him to Sea World that same week where he pet and fed the stingrays, are connections to that book, to the sea life creatures and to care of sea life creatures, these are connections in which he retains the information about stingrays on for the rest of his life. Life Long Learning at its' best!

As he continues to use and reuse this information, by telling others about his adventures and his love of stingrays, it reinforces the learning. This is how by making continuous connections, and allowing children to view their learning through their eyes to make those connections, rather than that we wish for them or that of which is imposed upon them, and then continuously utilizing what they have learned by expressing those connections in various ways, such as the way Matthew did, and other ways, that the learning "sticks in the brain" so to speak. It carries with us through our whole lives long.

Phase Three ~ Inclusivity of Learning

The third and final phase of Life Long Learning comes when we can view, with honestly and sincerely, *all* learning as equal ~ not holding one method, style, subject, or means of obtaining information above another. The term of Life Long Learning is now embraced fully as a method of homelearning that we utilize, because it is realized that since all of our children, regardless of method are no longer within a "schooling" environment, therefore homelearning is now embraced. We are also able to view school as a viable option out of choice only, not of demand, and we also see that the schooling environment, while it may be a choice that others make and embrace, that it may not be our choice at this time. If we or others choose it, then this is ok. If we or others do not choose it, then this is ok also. It is a realization that no one method of learning is right or wrong for us or another. It is just what works best for you. This inclusivity of learning, would then also apply to all different forms of learning approaches within the homelearning community.

As a Life Long Learner, there comes a time when inclusivity becomes the forethought of one's mind. Being a Life Long Learner, and embracing its' freedom, does not mean that we must shun or dislike every person who chooses to use curriculum, belongs to a charter, or uses any other form of homelearning or schooling for that matter. Clearly, it should be noted that these afore mentioned approaches, having gone through the previous two stages, do not make much sense and in no way would we wish to turn to these other approaches by the time we have reached phase three. However, as a whole, the homelearning community has yet to see Life Long Learning in its' glorious form and to completely embrace it for the wonderful style of homelearning it is. It becomes up to us then, should we choose, to share with others all we know of Life Long Learning to expand the consciousness of others, to help them to come to know that there is choice, as there is always choice.

Within homelearning, there is a wide range of homelearning styles yet out there. When you reach phase three, you can then come to encompass, appreciate, and embrace all learning, knowing that it is all a matter of choice when it comes to which form of homelearning each family provides their children. It is an acceptance that these methods, while we may or may not choose to utilize them, are all different forms falling under the same umbrella of homelearning and that we can all respect each other's choices even if we do not agree with these methods. We can in essence, agree to disagree and yet each person, each family will continue to have their own different forms of learning. Neither one is right nor wrong, it just is. It just is whatever each individual's, each family's path of learning is.

Inclusivity Within the Homelearning Community

At one point, a friend of mine and I saw this need to expand inclusivity within the homelearning community. This came to light as a direct result of the experiences that both of us shared in which we were excluded based upon the fact that we were one method of homelearning or another ~ being "excluded" based upon this fact alone, from what appeared to be on the surface as an inclusive group. This group that I speak of here along with many others in society today are choosing more and more to be exclusionary as a basis to state that they are somehow better than others if others do not choose to believe as they do. This again goes back to the "schooled" mentality of group segregation based upon the idea of an "I am better than you" scenario that I previously mentioned. I believe that although this type of mentality does indeed exist, this does not excuse our behavior towards one another in this modality, nor does it excuse our continued tolerance for it. Both this close friend of mine and I, seeing this need to break the mold surrounding exclusionary behavior, as well as, the need to speak out to show others that indeed there is another way, is how the inclusivity list on yahoo groups came to be envisioned and brought to fruition.

This group list unfortunately, turned into a list that has since gone by the wayside due to the fact that others on the list saw the group as a way to push forward their own political agendas, as to what homelearning should be and what it should not be, and whom should be allowed to be considered a homelearner and whom is not. To this, we were truly saddened, as that is not what inclusiveness is nor should be about in this world. Inclusiveness of Learning should be to include all forms of learning, no matter which way we learn. No one way is better than the other to learn at home, it is just what works best for each person, each family. There are many paths to homelearning, and they all lead to learning.

It is still our sincerest wish that we continue to provide a safe haven of inclusion for all in the homelearning community. My hope is that this book will be the bridge between the gaps. To reach out and to further continue to break away from the exclusionary stereotypes and ridiculing that is so prevalent with the homelearning community and society as a whole today, so as to provide a basis for all to be included no matter what. We *can* all coexist through this common bond we share and provide a safe haven to discuss issues without fear of one person or one form of homelearning being better than another. It is the including of all, excluding none and being accepted for what we choose to do in life and within the homelearning community is what we all seek.

Coming Full Circle

By phase three within the Life Long Learning process; we are in fact living and breathing Life Long Learning, inclusivity in learning, inclusivity in life. It then becomes such an intrinsic part of our everyday living that we cannot separate it from our lives, it becomes our lives. It becomes apart of our lives because we are now choosing for it to be apart of our lives effortlessly. It is not that we seek to "educate" as a part of learning, but we rather view everything in life as educational, as learning.

This may also be the time in which classes and/or instruction may wander back into your lives. At this point, no more or less weight is given to the learning that is happening in a Physics or Taekwondo class just because it is taking place within a classroom setting. A class, any class one chooses to take at this point, can the be considered as just another means of pursuing a passion, the making of connections to life and in life, of receiving information, knowledge, and wisdom on any given topic. It is then that you come to realize that learning can and does happen all the time and in all places, even in a classroom. We feel a sense of freedom in knowing that we do not need to be worried whether or not our children will pass trigonometry or whether they will be able to get into a good college, because they will if they choose to. We know that they will pursue their passions...well, passionately! And that each day will bring more connections and learning opportunities.

This is also when we begin to feel comfortable with effectively and confidently sharing Life Long Learning with others should we choose to. We feel open to the endless possibilities in our lives and in the lives of our children, so it then becomes a natural progression of things to want to share with others the freedom we have found. Discovering ways to reach out to the homelearning community is the next step in "paying the learning forward". Keep in mind, that to reach this phase is not something that can just happen over night. There is a level of trust and patience that one should develop and sustain, in order for these phases to come to fruition. One should go through the first two phases, which will seemingly blend one into the other, just as a woven blanket ~ soft and interconnected together that when complete will make a beautiful work of art. Just as the first piece of yarn needs to be started before the other pieces will fall into place, so too it is with the Life Long Learning phases. The first phase is that of the first piece of yarn, and the second phase cannot really be encompassed without the foundation and completion of the first, just as the third phase cannot be arrived at before and embraced before the second phase has been brought to completion.

For those of us that attended school, deschooling will always exist at a lower level throughout our lives. It will be a process that we will continue to struggle with and continue to transform. It is my vision, and that of a growing segment of our population that the next generation, that of our children, will not have this stage to work through. Our children, through our showing them the path, will be able to see all learning as inclusive and equal from the very beginning enabling their Life Long Learning to be less of a struggle than ours is. Now, this is not to say that this is how we envision things all the time, nor how we feel 1000% of the time either. There will be Life Long Learning days where we feel like our children have or are not learning anything and that this is not working. We all have our days, when we doubt what we are doing, that it is not all, as they say, a "bed of roses". There will be days too, when we will feel like we are all the back to phases one and two. Maybe it will be due to something someone may have said, or because of so and so's child making "honor roll" in their school or because we are just having a bad day in general. I myself, even now, still have those days as they are as much a part of being human.

The one thing that always brings me back to the peace, the freedom, and the happiness that is Life Long Learning are those what I call "little learning moments of love" that our children give us everyday. Most of the time, I spend my days in awe of how our three boys grow and learn, they inspire me to newer levels each day. But on those days when I am weary, I just stop. I just stop and take a look around me. I take a look around to see what *really* is ~ that could mean something as simple as watching Matthew over in his garden today, enjoying being the horticulturist he is ~ watering, planting, learning......or it could be Anthony, who comes in with his Magnetix creation and is imagining it to be a camera to take pictures with all over the house or a satellite that controls all of the televisions in the house or a mini CD player as he pretends to play music and listen to it or a video game player as he pretends to push buttons on it as if he is playing Nascar........or it could be Chris, who is at his computer working diligently on my website for this book and creating ideas for the pages of it in his ingenious use of a PC. I stop. I take the time to observe these awe inspiring children of mine and my husbands ~ to see how happy they are and how much they are really learning in life in those moments. Those are the moments when I truly know in my heart, in my soul, that Life Long Learning is worth it, and I need nothing more than that to show me.

~

The Quantum Leap ~ There are times when moving forward is not enough. There are times when you cannot just change what you do, how you speak and how you think about things. Sometimes, you have to change who you are. You need to pick both feet off the ground you tread and leap. ~ Unknown

It is our choices, Harry, that show what we truly are, far more than our abilities. ~ Albus Dumbledore

Chapter Three

Choice OR Decision,
Trust and Letting Go of Fears

In life, I am not big on defining or labeling things, or people for that matter, in a context that excludes anyone or anything. This is why defining things in life for the purpose of knowledge of what things in life mean, free from judgment, is the basis of where I am coming from within this chapter. In looking at the words Choice and Decision, I often wonder ~ what do these words really mean? How do they fit into the Life Long Learning spectrum? In looking at the word 'Decide', it comes from the root word 'cide'. This root word 'cide' means "to cut off". To cut off? Yikes! Does not sound very inviting to me! Whereby there are other words with this root word in it, such as, genocide, homicide, suicide, and so on. I do not know about you, but I do not wish to "cut off" anything within my life in that context or any other for that matter!

However, this is exactly what one does when "deciding" to do something, "deciding" to not do something, or anything with the implication of "decide" in it. When we "decide" something, we are picking whatever it is we are going to do, say, or where we are going to go etc. and "cutting off" all other possibilities, not looking at any and/or all other options. Now, let us look at the word choice. The word choice implies that you have viewed all possibilities and upon doing so, you simply choose to utilize one of the many possibilities before you. Choosing is a matter that gives birth to possibility, decision cuts off possibility. Within Life Long Learning then, we wish to provide our children and ourselves with the ability to choose ~To choose how, when, where, and why they will and we will learn. No one wishes for someone to decide for them, or "cut off" all possibility for themselves in their life. Children should be no exception and should also be allotted this ability as well.

The Point of Choice

So, you may ask ~ "What is the point of choosing?" Well, since we have already established that of the fact that in life, all of us wish to choose openly and freely without any possibilities being "cut off", therefore, we shall look to the movie *Matrix Revolutions* for the answer as to the point of choosing. This movie, of which the screenplay was written by the Wachowski Brothers, got the inspiration for this screenplay and subsequent movie, while taking a seminar series called "The Landmark Forum". If you should wish to have further information on Landmark Education, please refer to the back section of this book. In this seminar series, of which I have also taken, which is how I came to know of this information about the Matrix series, one of the topics of discussion during the seminar when I took it was that of choice and decision.

So, if you are to take a look at the movie Matrix Revolutions, in the end of the movie, Neo is asked by Agent Smith, "Why do you continue to do this Mr. Anderson?" to which Neo replies, "Because I choose to". Simply put, he chooses to. Nothing more and nothing less.

Our children, as we all do, choose what it is they wish to learn, simply because they do. In compulsory education, that choice is made for them, thereby it is not a choice, but a decision. Teachers, administrators, the government, parent all "decide" for children what, when, where, how, and why they learn. Why is that? Because as a societal whole, we choose to allow them to! Most people do not realize yet, that indeed there is another way. That our children can choose their own learning, much as we do ourselves.

The common belief and misconception sadly in our society says that children are not of the mindset, or maturity level, or experience level to be able to make informed choices for themselves. However, I disagree. The fact is that whether we realize it or not, or whether we choose to admit it or not, we have been making choices since the day we were born into this world. We chose when to cry for food as babies, we chose when we would walk, and we chose when we would talk. We were guided along the way, yes, by those whom loved and cared for us, but we are the ones whom chose these things. No one forced us to learn these modalities of life, we just did. Why? Because we chose to. So what makes others outside of ourselves feel they are so more in tuned to us than we are with ourselves, that they feel the need to make choices for us is a concept in this society I will never able to grasp.

Thus, how will our children ever learn if they have indeed made the supposed "right choice" if they are not able to do so for themselves? The only way for children or any one individual to learn is by doing it, by experiencing it for themselves. And if it is not the "right" choice, then they can start all over again choosing another path. We do this many times in our lives as adults. The fact that we are older than that of a child does not make that process any different. We as older individuals choose a path, and if it seems not to be working as we chose it to, we pick ourselves back up and travel a different path. One does not need to become an adult to all of the sudden know this concept. It was born with us.

The "Right" Choice

And what is the supposed "right choice" mean anyhow? Right choice for whom? Was it the right choice or wrong choice because someone else said so, or is it the right choice or wrong choice because **you** say so? No one but us can know for certain without any hesitation that the choices we make in our lives, whether it be which socks to put on or whether or not to get married and start a family, but us. You are the only one who can determine this; you are the only one who would know.

It is like the analogy of what a blueberry tastes like. I could sit here for days, months, years, until I became "blue" in the face (no pun intended here!) attempting to describe for you what a blueberry tastes like. I can be as descriptive and as imaginative as I could be, and you still would never know what a blueberry tastes like. That is, until you have tried it for yourself. Until you have the experience of that scrumptious little morsel, until you have lived it in your experience, it will only mean to you that of what it is to you, a description of what a blueberry tastes like. And the only way for you to experience it, **is** to experience it.

Others may offer their wisdom based upon their knowledge and their life experience, but ultimately, the only one who knows how it will all come out in the end is you because it is your life and you are living it. Their wisdom can prove to be invaluable, should you choose to utilize the same way that this person or persons lived their life, however, which path you will choose is ultimately up to you. It is not to say that their wisdom is "wrong" should we choose not to utilize it either. It is just merely that we viewed this wisdom, and chose now to utilize it, nothing more, and nothing less. Any judgments placed upon your choice of utilizing it or not after your choice, are that of another's judgment and should not influence your choice, if you have chosen because you choose to.

We were all given free will, and that free will was not given as a means to be taken away simply because you are deemed by society as a child and therefore know nothing by societal standards. By all accounts, there are children whom society would deem as smarter and wiser than their older counterparts, and of which these older counterparts could actually learn from, much more than the other way around in some instances. Free will was given to us at birth for a reason, for us to utilize it from birth. If it was meant to be given to us when we were older, than it would have been given then, not at birth.

So it is for our children. No one but each child individually will know if the choices they make to learn what they learn will be what is termed by others as the "right or wrong" thing to learn or if they should have done it this way or that, but our children. And it is only up to each individual, each child to choose then what is deemed as "right or wrong", not that of society's choice. To allow society to choose, rather than each individual is giving the power to society and taking it away from that person. Under the basis of free will that we were all given, no society, no one group, nor no one person has the right to do so. Yet, this is what society, governments, schools, and ultimately we as parents do to children by not allotting for choice. It is only when we let go of our need to be right, our belief that we know better another does what is best for them that true choice and true learning can emerge.

Guidance

This is not to say that you, as your child's parent, will not provide any means of learning for your children. Of course you most certainly do and will over the course of their lives. And that learning will not stop because they turn eighteen or because they move out, marry, and have a family of their own. This is why it is Life Long Learning, as this learning occurs from the day you were born until the day you leave this earth. Learning does not stop because of some magical number society "decides" it does, or because you are on your own. It occurs every minute of every day, your whole life through. Shoot, I am still learning from my parents every day, and my grandparents too!

The learning you will then provide will be in the form of guidance. Guidance comes from the word to guide, and to guide means to give a sense of direction. Therefore you provide a guiding direction with regard to what their passions, interests, observations, conversations, and experiences are. What they wish to explore, rather than something forced upon them, or "decided" for them by society, that they must struggle to "measure up" and conform to. It is the allowing of the choice of freedom of their own minds, so that they will be able to think for themselves and live life for themselves as they have always known since birth how to do.

So What of "Have to's"

I find the perception of "have to" quite amusing to be honest. No one **has** to do anything in this life that they do not **choose** to. Now, a lot of you will immediately disagree with me, saying, "Oh yes there are many things in this world we have to do, such as I have to go to work, and my children, well they just have to learn! If the do not learn, well they will become vegetables, unproductive members of society!" Well now, quite the contrary. We do not **have to** go to work. We choose to go to work. Of course, I know you are saying to me, to this book, and to yourself ~ "How can she possibly think in her right mind that I choose to go to work? If I had the choice, I would be on a cruise to Jamaica right now!" Again, you choose to work because maybe you do wish to go on that cruise and the money that you will make from your chosen career may make it so that you can go on that cruise to Jamaica. However, you do still have a choice. You might say, "No I do not have a choice", but by all accounts, you do have a choice. You **can choose not** to work. Of course, if you do make that choice, you may have to deal with the many consequences of making that choice; but nonetheless, you can choose not to go to work.

With our children, they do not **have to** learn. No one, but society, says that they have to learn. Now as to the argument that if they do not learn that they will become vegetables and unproductive members of society, I find this to be simply an absurd mindset. Absurd because learning is innate. There is never a single moment in time when we are not learning. It is a natural as breathing. So to say our children will not learn or that they have to learn or that they will become unproductive members in society if they do not learn, is to say that we do not breathe. Now if we are not breathing, then we are not of this planet, this world anymore, so we indeed are breathing, and yes we **are** learning. Now, will our children, being Life Long Learners, learn what they need to in order to be productive members of society? Oh yes, very much so, they will. How do we know this to be true? That is a matter of trust.

A Matter of Trust

One of the many things that you come to realize for yourself within Life Long Learning is the art of patience and trust. Patience in entrusting that your child will learn. Much as you wished, when your child was younger, that they would hit those all important "milestones" that everyone, including you, expect ~ we also need to realize that ~ being that each child is unique that learning may or may not occur within the time frame that "we" choose *or* the way "we" choose, or the way that "school" chooses, but it *will* happen. The proof that we are innate learning human beings exists in the mere fact that we were all able to crawl, stand, walk, and talk ~ all of those things and more ~ without ever being "taught" to do so. The beauty of it is, that children have their whole lives to learn.

How is it that we come to trust? Learning to trust our children is that of like learning to trust anything or anyone. It comes from a combination of factors. Trust does not come in time, as people always coin this phrase, "Oh it will come in time". No, trust is not a matter of a passage of time. It is a matter of a willingness to trust. It is a willingness to do so without a shred of doubt or hesitation.

How do we come to this place of encompassing trust in its entirety? We just do ~ the last factor in trust. We just do. It is a leap of faith. It is an inner knowing is something we all know well. Think back to the time you fell in love with the person you wished to marry or have be your life partner ~ in that moment, that first moment when you knew that this person was "the one", you knew beyond a shadow of a doubt. This is what trust in your child is. The trust beyond that shadow of a doubt that your child will learn all of what they need in this life.

The same holds true with that of our letting go of our fears over whether our children will learn or not, of whether or not Life Long Learning is the best approach for our children. Whenever I am in doubt, on those days when I am tired and weary and I think that our children are not learning anything, all I do is stop, take a deep breath or two, and look at my children. Really observe my children, and how they really have grown and how much they are learning. This and my complete faith and trust in our life as Life Long Learners, what it means, and all that is written in this book brings me back to the sense of peace and serenity that our children are happy and they are learning all they need to learn. It is what brings me back to that complete faith and trust in Life Long Learning. This is when the fear becomes obsolete again.

Rules

Pam Sorooshian, a homelearning mom and active member in the homelearning community wrote this when being asked of what her notions were on rules and limits, *"Arbitrary rules and limits have the characteristic that they entice children to think about how they can get around them and can even entice children to cheat and lie. I know a couple of really great Life Long Learning children whose parents set limits on their computer use time. The children used to get up in the middle of the night to use the computer while their parents were asleep. It is an unintended but very predictable side effect of rules and limits. These rules always set parents and children up as adversaries (the parents are setting the rules and the children are being required to obey them ~ these are adversarial positions) and can lead to children feeling guilty and sneaky when they inevitably bend or even outright break the rules. Avoiding that kind of possibility is one really good reason for not having rules or limits at all."*

I so love how Pam wrote these words because there is such truth in what she writes. It really sums up the concept of "rules" for me. Think back to when you were younger, a teenager maybe, did your parents absolutely forbid you to drink alcohol? Or maybe it was that they forbid you to not date or to hang out with "*that*" crowd, you know the group that was just such a bad influence? Now, did not the mere fact that they forbid you to not drink or hang out with that crowd, make you want to do so anyway? Of course it did! The mere fact in our existence is always to question why? with why not? We are wired as humans automatically to live out of unlimitless possibly.

Being in Infinite Agreement (IA)

Vicky Bennison, a homelearning mom once wrote *"I have found that children who do not have freedom of choice, or have been controlled, become angry. Adults do not see this anger, but other children often become targets because of it. I have had to explain to my child why another child, (who's mother is proud that he is not allowed to play violent video games, or use toy swords or guns) pushed him from the top of a very high hay pile, onto the hard ground, without warning, while laughing."*

How sad is this all because we constantly have to utter the word "no." Why is it that adults feel that they must exert their "power" over a child by utilizing the word no? I know what you are saying, that children must have that word of "no" for boundaries, rules, and structure, for without it, there would be such chaos. Actually the opposite is true. "No" forces chaos due to the simple fact that we are innately made to question why and no. It is one of the modalities of which we learn. In life are we not taught that the only way to learn is to ask questions, to ask why and why not? These are the very basic premises that are even "taught" in school for science. In a science class ~ in order to do experiments, one needs to ask the questions of why and no, along with other questions in order to work through any hypothesis. Yet, it is these very questions, that we then are punishing our children for asking, therefore we are punishing their learning.

When as a Life Long Learning family we come to respect our children as individuals, as people, that the factors such as rules, boundaries, and structure cease to exist. We can view children's needs as inconvenient for us or we can view them as people who need our assistance doing what they want to do, just as when we need help with something we need to do.

As adults, should we choose to create a sculpture out of clay, then we would then go and buy clay. If we wish to go out for a spaghetti dinner, then we will drive to our nearest Italian restaurant. If, as we often ask of children, we had to ask for and obtain permission from say our husband or wife to drive the car or buy the clay or if we had to somehow convince our husband or wife why it was a good idea to go dinner, then it would change our relationship knowing that they had the power to grant or deny our request based upon what *they* felt was important, of what their perception of important is at that moment. It would then be, a lack of their entrusting us to not only know how to make a choice, but of also understanding our own needs. Thus we would feel not worthy of making choices and then this would be a form of control. However, this is what we are doing when we are not respecting our children enough to trust that they can make choices and that they do understand their own needs as well as the needs of others.

As a parent, you learn to choose your battles when it comes to giving choice back into our children's hands. The question is what is more important? Is our need to take care of "things" around the house more important than a fun time spent playing and learning with our children? Is our need for "control" more important than loving and respecting our child? If we wish for our children to respect us, we need to respect them, as respects works both ways. In order to complete the circle of respect, half must come from each ~ half from you, half from your child.

In providing this complete circle of respect and choice, think about the memories and the learning connection you are creating with your children when you are with them in the now. Now is all we have, in this moment, and then the next. When we can be our children's partner, we are helping them to get what they want in and out of life. In this way we are providing the opening for unlimitless possibilities together rather than being a barrier that opens or closes according to our wishes for them. It is important to acknowledge and believe that our children will not make the same choices we will in life. We need to respect that what they have to say and do is important not only to us, but to life, and to the world, not of what we judge to be important. As Joyce Fetteroll stated, when speaking on this topic ~

"Children do not have the same needs as we do. If we want them to respect our needs then we need to offer them respect of theirs. Our children are unique people and they are not the age we are so their needs are unique. It is not our job to raise them to need what we need ~ they will have adult needs when they are of adult age ~ but to model how to respect others needs by respecting theirs. What is helpful is to recognize that what we think is important does not look important at all to children. We cannot make them understand how important it is. We can make them act as though they understand by making them comply with what we want. But that is not respect. That is control. If we want them to respect needs they do not understand, then we need to respect their needs we do not understand. It will not be an equal give and take for years and years, but eventually as the cognitive ability to understand someone's needs as separate from their own grows, as they build up a feeling of being respected, children will offer in return what has been given to them."

And then some! In some cases ten times over! I know that our own children, even at the ages they are now, have for years given respect to myself, my husband, and others simply due to the fact that we respect them and treat them as equals in the sense of deserving the same courtesies and the same extension of valuing them as individuals as they do of us. Aaron and I are often complimented by others observing or connecting with our children. People so often admire how respectful and polite our children are to them and others. In fact my Aunt this past Christmas commented to my mother about what perfect little respectful angels our children were that night. Now of course, they are far from angels as they do have their moments just as we all do. However, I was beaming with pride knowing that my children were that evening as they so often are respectful people. This does not come from us pounding respect into their heads, or demanding it from them and not returning it to them. It comes from a mutual respect built upon what Joyce so eloquently writes of.

There are several ways that one can say yes or a variation of yes. For example, you can say "Yes, we can do go there in about 20 minutes when I have finished what I am doing here. If you would like to give me a hand, then I can be done even sooner." Or "Yes, you can buy that. Let's think up ways you could save up or earn the *GEE* to buy this, or if you have at least half of the *GEE* then I will come up with the other half." I explain what *GEE* is more in-depth in chapter six. "Yes, we can do that in a little while, say after I take a nap as right now I am about to drop from exhaustion." Another way is just a simple *Y E S*, and then doing or going to where you were asked about.

It is in utilizing IA or Infinite Agreement, whereby replying with a yes or a variation of yes, that a sense of calmness begins to fill the air. The uttering of this three-letter word and the phrases associated with it, have a soothing effect upon the brain. It is also in sync with our natural innate ability to learn as human beings. Saying yes, opens the pathway to discovery. You might be asking me something along the lines of "If I say yes *all* the time, am I not just being a permissive parent, allowing my children to run all over me?" Contrary to this myth, saying yes actually gives way to a surreal sense of peace in your life and in that of your home. Arguing as to why one cannot do something or go somewhere or be with someone ceases to exist, as well as, does sneaking around and hiding things behind each other's backs. It builds a bond of trust between all. The trust is then exemplified when we follow through on that yes not from just saying it, but by actually doing as we say we will, which builds and models integrity. Trust cannot be built with anyone in life, our children included if we say yes and do not keep true to my word. Integrity builds trust.

Family

One of our biggest concerns when embarking upon being a Life Long Learning family, may be that of others reactions to our approach. And no one knows how to push our proverbial buttons better than our friends and family. Friends do, although I find that most friends seem to be more accepting of our lives being our own than that of our families. It seems that for some reason, family members at times feel that they know what is best for you and your children. They sometimes tend to forget that they do not live our lives; therefore they could not possibly know what is best for us and our children, as they are not us and they are not our children.

I refer you to the previous contents of this chapter in aiding you to somehow handle the issue of when family members or other people just do not seem to "get it", as in as much as this chapter applies to us with our own children, so too does this chapter apply to that of how our family members view us. Heck, you might even wish to invite them to read this whole book, or other related books on learning or homelearning to assist in smoothing the transition. I have a recommended list of reading material at the end of this book.

One thing I have learned however is that you cannot force anyone to "convert to your way of thinking and believing". Try as you might, we cannot change others. We only have control over that which has to do with ourselves. Therefore, as with anything in life, one needs to come to accept that to force change upon another is impossible. What is in the realm of possibility is not that of transforming others, but in transforming yourself and in how you view your friends and family, that when you resonate in a vibration of what it is that you believe in, that people can and often will come to embrace it as well. One is invited also to accept the fact that people are as they are and we need to be ok with the fact that should someone never choose to embrace the Life Long Learning approach, that this is ok too. That we are not in need of another's approval to live our lives; to grow and to learn with our children as we choose to. The only approval that is needed is that of ourselves.

What Do You Say?

A friend of mine, Susan Nowicke, once wrote about her views on Life Long Learning ~

"Life Long Learning is like a garden ~ you prepare the soil, plant the seeds, water & feed them ~ and for some time you may see nothing ~ but much is going on under ground. You do not scrap the garden when you do not see immediate results. Provided you care for the newly sown garden ~ you know deep down in the soil ~ changes are occurring ~ the seed germinates and pushes it's stalk toward the sky ~ then one day you walk out and the garden is full of little green sprouts! But your work is not done! For now you must still care for these tender stalks before you see them bear fruit ~ and sometimes that means a great deal of waiting. During that wait you water and

feed the sprouts, weed the garden bed and protect them from pests and intruders ~ then finally, after much time and care ~ fruit is put forth. Life Long Learning often brings concern to parents and those around you because they do not realize that much is going on "underground" ~ deep inside the child ~ but one day ~ if the child is nurtured and cared for ~ fed and protected from pests (naysayers, labelers, and other non-supportive parties) then they will blossom and bear fruit ~ and that fruit will be so very sweet."

Susan's analogy just brings tears to my eyes. It is such a beautiful way to bring into being Life Long Learning. What is it then that one does say to a family member, friend, or other individuals about our Life Long Learning approach? I have come to understand that when we live the life that we choose, there are times that others, such as that of our family and friends, do not understand the path we have chosen because we have not presented it in a way that they can resonate with and grasp.

For instance, when speaking with my family, I might say that today that our boys learned that of multiplication, division, percentages, and fractions. Now, placed in that context, my family would be able to grasp these math concepts that they are learning based upon the language that they know and can identify with. To another fellow Life Long Learner, however, I might wish to put it in another context. That of something like this ~ "WOW! You know today that our boys and I played this really awesome baseball game and in it we took the batting averages, came up with certain percentages, then added, and subtracted them to play this game like playing a baseball game out on a grass field with the boys. We did so because it was raining and we could not go out to play baseball. What a fun learning experience it was too, the game was not only great but the directions were also a learning challenge too".

Within these examples here, I was able to ~ without going into much detail about the logistics of a game where a family member might not be able to grasp the concept of learning taking place and without presenting it in such a language that my family does not know or understand ~ I was able to still explain to my family the learning that our children did do that day.

Family members will often need this type of an explanation within this context to help them to see that your children are learning and what they are learning. A lot of times family members and friends may have a hard time viewing learning in the manner that learning is all around us and that learning is in everything we do. By using this method of standardization within what I like to call "schoolease", we are able to place our loved ones minds at just as the word implies, at ease.

Close Encounters of the Family Kind!

There will be times, in fact, when our families and friends, as much as we love them and as much as we wish them to, they simply do not grasp the Life Long Learning methodology. When this occurs, it somehow feels like Close Encounters of the Family Kind! Our family members may become upset with us and attempt to derail our bliss by seeming to know better than we do on what is best for our children and for us, and attempt to voice that, no holds barred to us.

It is in these times of family and friendship uncertainty, when the strength of our resolve is tested. It is in these times that we must respectfully request that our family and friends, while they may feel that they know what is best for us, and may very well be concerned that we are "doing right" by ourselves and our children, that they respect our choice to be a Life Long Learning family. That even if they do not agree with our approach, we respectfully ask that they give unconditional love and support, just as we do of them, even if we do not agree with what they may do or not do with their lives.

It is not our job or theirs to judge whether or not something is right or wrong for someone else's life. What may have been good for our family or friends may or may not be for you, as each individual is unique and as such each person's life is going to be unique. We may have similar experiences and stories to share, but each person's paths are unique. As such with this book, if you read this book, and determine that being a Life Long Learning family will not work for you, then you will choose your own path, as you so choose it to be. My hope is that you will see all the benefits of the Life Long Learning modality, and embrace it, and tweak it to how it fits your life and your family.

So as to our family and friends, if they do not wish to embrace the Life Long Learning philosophy in whole or in part, then we can still love them for who they are and accept that we can agree to disagree. We can respect and honor their feelings, while still honoring that of who we are without anyone having to "change" to any one way of thinking. We cannot change someone or what someone thinks or feels, we can only change ourselves and our reactions to others. With strength in our resolve, even when that resolve is tested, if we, all of us children and adults alike, hold true to what we feel is the best for us each as individuals and as a family, without judgment of others not having those same beliefs or holding those same truths as we do, then we can all coexist happily free from hurt and pain and within infinite possibility.

What about Being a Life Long Learning Family while working full time? Can it be done?

Some may ask, how can we be a Life Long Learning when I am, or my spouse and I are working full time at professional jobs? I will tell you that my husband Aaron and I work full time jobs as well both of us. It depends on what you consider a professional job I suppose. Both my husband and I work and we are a Life Long Learning homelearning family of three. My husband works in an office environment about 60 miles one way away from where we live and myself I am a fulltime writer, lecturer on homelearning and other topics, published author (my second book to be released in the next year), and the director of my own Spiritual Center which holds weekly classes among other events. And I do all of this from home working professionally fulltime from home while we are still a Life Long Learning homelearning family. So you could say that we have experienced what we may call as success in homelearning our three boys and both of us working fulltime.

Managing is rather easy actually as we are a pretty go with the flow type of family. Learning with us occurs 24/7 really anytime and anywhere. This book if you so choose to utilize the wisdom within its pages, can assist you in getting started on homelearning and to see just how easy it can be, even with working fulltime! If we can do it, I am confident you can too! Take advantage of any and all resources available to you if you really desire to be a Life Long Learning homelearning family. This can be anything from hiring a nanny if you can afford one, to asking relatives to assist during the day, to co-op sharing with another homelearning family, to bringing your child to work with you if your company allows it, to telecommuting, to owning your own business where you can work from home ~ the possibilities are infinite! It can work, it really is about just how much you desire to provide a homelearning environment for your children and how flexible you are willing to be to provide that. Remember, that with Life Long Learning homelearning, learning is free from any "have to's" of being within certain time frames and schedules during any given day.

Learning can and does occur 24/7 whenever and wherever we and our children choose it to!

Life Long Learning and the Single Parent

What about Being a Life Long Learning Family while being a single parent? Can it be done? First let me say that I can surely understand where the single parent comes from. I was a single parent for the first 2 years and 9 months of our oldest sons Chris's life before marrying my husband our boys' daddy and wonderful hubby he is too! And also, I will say that there was a time several years ago when I was going to be possibly be facing the real possibility of being a single parent with all three of our boys as we hit a very rocky patch in our marriage and had been separated for 4 months and almost divorced.

Of course, yes, things are wonderful in our marriage now, and one can consider this to be a learning experience for all of us. My point in writing this is to let the single parents out there know that I understand where they are in their lives right now as albeit maybe for only a short time, I still have had the same experience and can understand what a single mom goes through within homelearning among many other things. Thus, I would like to say that YES, yes, homelearning as a Life Long Learning family can be accomplished even as a single parent. There are many options available to us today to assist us with being a Life Long Learning family. Life Long Learning is really for all ~ all families and all people and children of this earth, as there are infinitely various types, shapes, and sizes of families and of people on this earth.

I can tell you that Life Long Learning can definitely be done as a single parent. And it need not be done in "normal school hours" either. Life Long Learning is learning 24 hours a day 7 days a week within this concept we know as time here on this earth. There are no time limits or restrictions on the when, where, or how of learning, which is what makes Life Long Learning so unique and so wonderful; and yet at the same time, so very natural. The same ideas and concepts that I speak about here within this book are the very ones that can be utilized no matter if you are a single mom or married or whatever type of family life you embrace.

Thus, I invite you as a single parent to incorporate learning into everything you do. If you have chosen that this Saturday you are going to work on fixing the toilet, then this is the day that your child can learn about plumbing. If its your shopping day, have your child help to plan nutritious meals, shop for the best buys (explaining what parts of the plant or animal the food comes from), and later on help cook. (That covers what we would call in schooling or educational terms as health science, economics, biology, and the physics of cooking -- even handwriting, if they wrote out the list!)

Within Life Long Learning as a single parent or in any form of life we have, we are free from having to learn everything ALL at once or having to take this on all by ourselves. Just as we do Aaron, the boys, and I here as a Life Long Learning family, you can have others you know who have skills in areas that your children wish to learn and then trade or barter things with them in exchange for learning with your children. Our son Chris does this alot in instructing other children in homelearning families on the uses of the computer. We trade with other people in life of learning so that we all can learn. Shoot, even if you have a vet, the vet can help your child to learn about the life cycle of fleas!

If you find due to custody issues as I almost did (as I did look into and consider this as well at one point and I know many people who do and have done this) that if you are required by your state, country, or by your ex spouse to go with a charter so that they feel comfortable that your child is learning "something" by their standards rather than by what you child wishes to learn; then do so; finding as flexible of a charter as possible so that you can still incorporate with the Life Long Learning into your life and still fulfill the ex spouse's wishes. Also a single parent can find a good sitter, enlist relatives, and friends to instruct your child occasionally on whatever it is they like best ~ doing just a little each night, and be a Life Long Learning family on weekends or whenever you have your child with you. One can also encourage your child to read a lot and have materials around for 'projects,' and, yes, you can be a Life Long Learning family ~ and relatively cheaply, too.

This is what one Homelearning mom wrote to me once:

"As a single parent who choose Life Long Learning as a way of homelearning for my children, the most common question I get asked is, "How do you do it?" It is really very simple. I do it by one day and one moment at a time. Having said that, raising and providing a Life Long Learning homelearning environment for my children as a single parent is really a daily walk of balance, faith, and love. It is rarely easy, but it can be done.

I have faced the normal struggles I find many homelearning families face when choosing home education, and I face the same questions: "What do I use for a curriculum?" "Am I really qualified to help my children learn what they wish to?" and of course, "What about socialization?" This to me is the biggest laugh I get, because I've never met (I'm not saying they don't exist, only that I've never met) a poorly socialized homelearning child. I have however, met many children that I wish "lacked" the social skills our public schools seem to instill in our children. I feel like I can go to any store and just look at how the child is interacting with those around him and know how lucky I am to have chosen this way of life for our family and how I so hope the same for all families one day. In addition to the normal issues homelearning families face, single parents often face the additional hurdle of balancing the need to earn an income with the need to be at home with the children. The work-from-home opportunities are growing, thanks to technology. Many often need to accept help from government welfare and social service agencies at least initially. I've had times where I've received welfare, and others when I've been self-employed. I've worked as a family childcare provider, which was an excellent fit with our homelearning in the beginning. Now I tutor and work as a freelance writer. We have a Life Long Learning environment that fits within our family and my working. For one day to the next it may be different, and that is ok, as learning happens all the time free from schedules and time variables. We do what works for us in the moment, in that day, in that week, in that month. This leaves a way for me to be able to work, still be with my children, and provide learning for all of us."

Flexibility is the key to making homelearning (Life Long Learning) work as a single parent. What works for me may be free from working for you. Likewise, what works today may be free from working tomorrow, next week, or next year. As the children grow, change, and learn, so do the demands on the single parent. Older children may be able to work more independently and help more around the house, freeing up the parent to work more hours.

I also have many resources of learning that can be adapted to fit for the Life Long Learning single parent and for all parents in the back of this book, as well as, regular updates to our Life Long Learning website under the free stuff and links webpages. All of these ideas and infinitely others, are open and adaptable to any situation whether you are a Life Long Learning single parent, a grandma Life Long Learning with your grandchildren with deceased parents, or a family with a mommy and a daddy at home. This is the beauty of Life Long Learning is that it is truly for All, regardless of your life path.

These resources and inspiration that I have found in my extensive research for single parents out there to see that YES you can be a Life Long Learning family ~ As a Single Parent or as any form of family life you have. Some of the links here are from various homelearning options and backgrounds, however, all of the ideas and concepts here that can easily be applied to Life Long Learning. It is my fondest and dearest wish that this wisdom and resources provided in the back of this book and on the Life Long Learning website, help to inspire you to see that YES Life Long Learning is possible for everyone, it is unlimitless!

~

Hit the Road ~ Getting to where you need to be is an important step. Even more important is getting out of your space and onto the road. ~ Unknown

You cannot teach a man anything; you can only help him to find it within himself ~ Galileo

Chapter Four

Strategies for Life Long Learning

While this whole book is dedicated to various strategies for Life Long Learning, I thought a chapter on some more specifics here was needed. There are many life strategies that evolve around, in, and through Life Long Learning. Many will say that these are day-to-day issues that children and parents have to just "deal" with in life. I prefer to think of them in terms of life strategies. Why? The term "issues" seem to give the view or connotation that things in life are nothing more than pesky problems that we just want to "do away" with. Now I ask you really ~ do we, as life long learners, or at any point in our lives wish to "do away with" our children? Do we wish to just "do away" with issues or do we wish to rather grow and transform our lives through the various scenarios that happen to along within it?

It seems to be that parents of the children who are in this institutional learning environment are all too delighted once their child is "of school age". I must admit, regretfully, I was one of those moms, who was just all too happy to have "free time" once all of my children were of school age. That last all of a few months, and then I came to wonder....Why am I so happy about "getting rid of" my children? Was it not the whole point in **having our children** to **BE** with them ~ to live with them, learn with them, and from them, and them from me, enjoy them, and love them?

Balancing and Rejuenation

Now, while I must admit, there are times when I just need a break. After all I am human, just like anyone else. Sometimes, just like anyone else might, I need some time down time to regroup, to put myself back in balance. We all need this balance within our lives to help center us and make us more energized to work with and through life and our everyday interactions with others. It is what makes us more loving as mothers and fathers ~ if we are able to take care of our own spiritual, emotional, physical, and personal needs, we are then rejuvenated back into being the inspirational, loving parents we are. However, this is not to say that we **must** or **have to** have this break every single day or for such prolonged periods of time. Nor is that to say that I cannot have a simple break of an hour to myself, while my children are still physically here within the same space as I am in. I can very easily accomplish this by going to another room and before doing so, explaining to our children that "Mommy needs so down time to relax". It is a matter of choice in how we wish to accomplish this.

Another way I have learned to approach this, is to be enthralled in what it is I wish to do for my down time ~ be it reading a book, working on my computer, sitting to watch a show on the television, or just a having a cup of tea ~ all while my children are in the room with me. There becomes after a time, once you have moved seamlessly through the phases of Life Long Learning, where a natural rhythm seems to just effortlessly flow like a river, to where your children just instinctively know when you wish to have that down time.

With our own children, I have found that when I am involved in something, there can be times when they just instinctively know that I need my quiet time and they will respond by doing one of several things ~ either they will leave the room I am in to pursue that of their own interests, stay with me in the room I am in and pursue a quiet interest sitting or laying near me, or there are even times when our boys will wish to cuddle with me and just "Be" with me within the space of calmness and quietness. There are times too, when I just need to state aloud that I need a quiet space and then I ask if they can leave the room or quietly engage in something of their interest while I am taking the time I need to focus and center myself.

It seems that the more time has passed though, the more in-tuned to each other we have become as a family. We can feel or sense when one or more of us need space and with just the normal ebb and flow of life, we are able to find that balance with ease. I admit, when the children were smaller, this was somewhat difficult to accomplish, being that that were more dependent on me for things such as snacks and the like, however, as they have gotten older and their independence grows and their willingness to go out on a limb and try something new or attempt to do something that they have never done before, this too has helped make life more balanced.

What About Curriculum?

As far as curriculum goes, our curriculum is life. Matthew is looking into learning Visual Basic Computer Programming and C++ Computer Programming, as well as learning website design. Our youngest Anthony is learning website design as well. Our oldest Chris is helping to instruct them, simply because he has learned so much of the computer himself and chooses to assist our family with this learning. We also buy, rent, or borrow the software and books needed relative to this learning. So curriculum per se is free from being a set of structured ideas to follow based upon someone else's idea of what our kids should learn but rather it is books, resources, software, internet, library, hands on learning materials (such as the planting seeds we just purchased at our local store to learn of what we could plant for food crops now and what we would need to wait to plant, and then planting them) or people we can talk to an learn from (such as Matthew learning just recently how to be in a hitting stance for baseball from another friend who is on a baseball team) and so many other possibilities, that are geared to their interest and within those resources the other learning of what we call subjects such as math, reading, science and such are learned through these resources.

In utilizing life as our curriculum, or boys are then able to choose what it is from a plethora of learning options as to what it is they wish to learn about in life. Then we as a family brainstorm, explore, gather, and utilize all possibilities that are available to us. This form of learning is free from the age restrictions and scope of possibilities that are currently available within the compulsory educational environment. Anything and everything that our children wish to lean is then at our fingertips, rather than a certain set box of particular learning materials. We then choose our learning materials based upon what it is our children are interested in or passionate about, rather than by some grade, age, or material standards. We choose the material related to the passion and interest rather than letting the material dictate to our children their passion and interest.

I know this may be free from the answer that one is looking for when searching for a set thing called curriculum. However, if we choose to view it from this other perspective, then we are providing learning for our children that is unlimited possibilities rather than a set of boxed curriculum that instructs from someone else's idea of what they should learn. It places the learning then within what they are passionate in learning about and opens the door to the infinite possibilities of learning within what they are passionate about and what they want to learn. And it gives us an opportunity to explore infinite possibilities in learning together with our children and of stepping outside of the curriculum box to learn. Life once we are outside of the compulsory educational influence, whether it be through homelearning, or for those of us whom did go all the way through twelve plus years of school and are now adults, learning is free from being in a set box of certain parameters. As adults, we know that we learn free from any curriculum other than the one we choose relative to our interests and passions And children should be given this same freedom. Learning is available to us through life in its many infinite forms, all we are being requested to do is check them out, and learn from them.

Another bonus to using the world and life as our curriculum is the money that you save. We have saved quite a bit of money since our children are free from being in the schooling environment. When our boys were in school, it was much more costly to be in school or in buying curriculum and doing the whole school at home thing, relative to the amount of money (or GEE ~ Green Energy Exchange which I speak of later in this book) we spend now. I remember when our children went to school and before the first day even started we had to spend $70 per child (and we have three boys) just on school supplies! In addition to that school clothes which even at thrift store prices is a lot for three growing boys and other things such as like field trips, gas to and from school, fund raisers, and other related events etc. Now with this money free, we are able to purchase resources, borrow, or rent resources relative to their passions and interests free from having to spend as much money. Something worth thinking about!

Seizing the Moment

When does learning occur? As a Life Long Learning family, we know that learning occurs in every moment. It is in seeing the moments and seizing the moments as opportunities for learning that create love of learning, independence, and interconnection in our children's lives.

As adults, when we wish to learn something, do we not throw ourselves right into whatever that is we wish to learn? A wonderful example of this is when our children were young. I can remember each one of our boys coming to us at the age of 2 or 3 with the broom in one hand and the dustpan in the other and wanting to learn how to sweep just like they saw mommy and daddy doing. I can remember in each instance, allowing our children to sweep, and showing them how to do so, step by step. We even went out and got from the thrift store and our local department store, their own size broom and dustpan so that they may sweep while we were sweeping with them because the other broom they said was too heavy for them and they wanted something they could hold and help us with without falling over or dropping it from its weight. This gave us bonding time together, a way for our children to learn something that they wanted to in that very moment, and a knowing that they are independent and they can do such a task brightens their day and ours!:) Now, as the boys are older, they enjoy helping mom clean the house, or putting away the groceries, or cooking, or assisting others with these tasks because of our taking the time to help them learn in the moment that they desired to learn, in seizing the moment.

Now, some parents natural inclination is that "Oh it's going to take too much time, I need to do this, you are too young and cannot do this yet, thank you honey" and we take the broom from their hands, shoo them off into another room to watch TV, or to "get out of our hair" so to speak and we then take care of the task at hand, whether it be sweep, cooking, whatever it is in that moment that our children expresses an interest in learning. Our natural inclination then is that "I will take care of it, I will do a better job and I am faster than you". We all have had moments like this with our children. As long as we have the inclination that we can take care of it, that we will do a better job, and that we are faster than our children, then we in essence cripple our children because we shut them down and we wonder why then when later on then when they are 7, 8, or 9 and then we hand them a broom, or ask them to help with making dinner and such, they are free from being interested then and choose to be free from learning or helping and we wonder why, often getting angry or frustrated at our children for not wanting to or at their making a fuss about helping.

What we are being asked to recognize is that when our children comes to us wanting to learn to sweep, that means that they are ready to learn how to sweep, or learn a new computer programming language or whatever it is that they are wanting to learn in that moment. The thing is, if we take the time with our children in each moment to seize and enjoy the process of learning when they come to us with whatever it is they desire to learn in that moment then our children will then know whatever it is that they are desiring to learn, and then years down the road, which we may not see in that moment, we will have a children who is in love with learning anything and everything, independent, and interconnected with us and the world. It is in allowing our own children's love of learning and potential to be independent and to want to participate to grow and facilitate themselves and our family.

If a task seems to be too large for our children or even for us in that given moment to learn, then we can do what it is we do when we are desiring to learn something, we can break up into steps. One step in each moment at a time, slowly and carefully, until pretty soon, the get it! Then we can go onto the next step and the next. So get that smaller size broom if you need to, get that step stool, find and get whatever resources (and there are infinite ways to get resources either free or inexpensively if need be. I invite you to use your imagination and creativity with your children to find ways to get what it is that you need to learn, I know having three kids that I am always searching for a bargain) you need to allow your children to sweep, or peel the potatoes and carrots for dinner, or type on the computer and then enjoy the process, and the amazement and awe-inspiring wonder that enfolds before us as we are learning together with our children. Learning in this way also inspires a spirit of service within your family, so that as they grow there is a natural flow to your family and to life, free from having to push or force any learning or helping with the house work and such.

I have parents say to me all the time, "Gee you know my children LOVED to help with housework and such when they were younger and now that they are x age, they want nothing to do with helping me and I feel frustrated having to do ALL this stuff myself" To which I always ask them then "What was your reaction when they were younger and wanted to help?" If it was of the reaction that I described earlier of "I can take care of it, that I will do a better job, and that I am faster than you" is it any wonder then why you are tired and frustrated and are free from having assistance and free from having a children who wish to be of service, who want to help and who want to earn.

Is it hard at times? Sure, I know it is, especially when you are running around crazy with your kids and also if they are younger. I know what this is like as I had our children all three of them 7 and under for a time. Even now, at the age they are, while it is "easier" in some ways as I do have the help, but it also would be what others may consider as "too time consuming" having to stop and learn and grow with our children. For me though, what better way to enjoy the process of learning and of life with your children than in this way. Is this not the reason we have our children?

Can you start this process at anytime, even if they are older now and you were once living the way of "I can take care of it, that I will do a better job, and that I am faster than you"? Yes, we can begin, because really we are free from beginning anything, as the wisdom in being this has always been with us, it is that we somehow forgot about it and it takes a reminder of the messages in this article to wake us up to this process to continue what it is we may have been doing when they were younger or saw someone else doing with their children. How to begin or remember this? By allowing our children the space to come to us with a desire to learn whatever it is that they choose to learn, and then us taking the opportunity to seize the moment to learn with them, to show them, or to find the resources and learn together with them through those resources of what it is they desire to learn in that moment. What better moment, than this present moment to begin or remember in this very moment?

Will they do it perfect the first time? No. Did each of our boys sweep in what is called "correctly" the first times they did it? No. Do we as adults, learn something "right" the first time we learn it? Most likely No. And is it going to cost us what we believe as our time to assist our children in learning? Yes, it will. It was within taking the moments, moment by moment, even if it is a thousand moments, to show them, to help them to learn to sweep those crumbs into the dustpan and the elation on our children's face when they say "I did it!" that is all the "payment" we need. Our natural inclination is to rather than take opportunity to seize these moments to rather say that I am free from having enough time, I have such and such to do or here to go etc. but what could be more important than seizing the moment in each and every moment to learn with our children? What it all comes down to, which is what I speak about in the Life Long Learning Book is, how you approach life, learning and how we approach our children. If you choose to approach life and learn from a perspective of drudge and drudgery, then this is what will manifest for you in your life. If we view life, learning, and our children from and for the wonderous awe-inspiring beautiful things and being that they are, then we will greet each moment with that same wonder, inspiration, and beauty that they bring to us.

There is a song I like to sing that is from the Disneyland ride of Pirates of the Caribbean, with the words changed a bit ~ "Yo ho ho, a mommy's life for me" or "Yo ho ho, a Life Long Learning Life for me" or "Yo ho ho a Life Long Learning Life for all"! So whatever it takes to get you inspired in life to enjoy and learn from it with your children then let that flow of inspiration take you where it is that you and your children wish to go. Children know this, this is why you see children learning, playing and loving life always.

Why are they in this state? Because they live in a constant state of being grateful for everything in their lives. I invite you in those moments of drudgery to sit down and write a list of all that you are grateful for. You will be amazed at how much we are grateful for but tend to forget about in the perceived drudgery of life and how much having an attitude of gratitude shifts our perspective! There is truly **so** much we can learn from our children.

Our children are like gifts, presents that we open them when they are born and open them through life and watch and marvel at what comes out. If we have a vision for what we desire and who we are being in life and then make choices based on that vision, and if we have and our children have a vision of the man or woman that our children will grow to be and who is in the making in this very moment, then we will and they will make choices based on that vision of who we are and they are choosing to be, then we can watch the enfoldment of that gift in utter amazement and joy. We spend so much time thinking about, planning, and saving for college for our children what if we were to place that same emphasis instead on who we are and who are children are being in the moment and making choices based upon that and BEing then in the moment. Free from placing our children in a box, but open to the infinite possibilities of who are children is being in any given moment. Allowing them to show what gifts and talents they have and support them in their own individual ways of being.

If we have the vision that our children are the children that they wish for themselves to be and that they are happy in each moment with who they are being and what it is that they choose in their life experience, even if it is free from being what it is we may wish for them, then this is what matters. Because we all have, including our children, Divine Free Choice or Divine Free Will and even if our children grow to be other than what it is that we desire for them to be, it is their choice to be whom they are being in each moment just as it is ours, and if they are happy, then this can be our fondest wish for our children. I know it is for me with our children. For me, I choose the choice that I am free from anywhere I have to go, or anything I have to do, that is more important to me than our children and seizing the moment to learn and **BE** with our children within our visions whatever they may be for all of our lives. For me, I choose to be in and have an attitude of gratitude in every moment. When the invitation is brought forth from our children to me, I graciously, gratefully, and enthusiastically accept it and the party of learning begins. I watch then and am along side them in the enfoldment of the gift of who they are, which inspires me to be who I am. Do you choose to accept your children's next invitation to seizing the moment in learning?

Independence

Independence is one of the major keys in Life Long Learning, and in life in general. I believe that we, as Life Long Learners, and in our role as our children's guides, if you will, that we should foster independence within our children. We should not place limits upon our children in terms of restricting their abilities based upon our fear and beliefs. We often fear that our children our too young, or will get hurt, or we believe that they simply cannot do a task the way in which we wish them to do so. Therefore we will make statements such as, "Oh you cannot do that, it is too hard for you" or "Here let me do that for you". If we are saying these things in a way in which we are responding to a request for help from our children, then that is one thing.

However, if this is not the case, then such statements only serve to show our children that we feel them to be less competent and cannot complete a certain task. This then may lead them to a life similar to that of a schooling environment in that they will simply come to a point where they stop trying to doing things, or trying new things simply because their self worth and self-esteem is so low that they feel they cannot do something. Thus, later in life, as teenagers and adults, our children will then grow to expect that someone else will always be there to do something for them, rather than looking within and utilizing the power within their own being to transform their lives.

This begets a lifetime of problems with lack of personal responsibility for one's own life and the consequences that arise out of the choices that they make. Rather than taking responsibility, they look for someone else or something else to blame when troubles arise in their lives. Also, the opposite can be said along the lines of taking personal responsibility for one's own accomplishments. Children who tend to have things done for them their whole lives and not allowed to experience life fully without someone doing it for them, also have a hard time acknowledging when they have truly accomplished something in their lives. They will tend to look for outside persons or circumstances to take credit for what was really their genius.

So rather than inhibit, we should encourage. In truth, what will it hurt if our children do not do it "right" as we perceive they should? Is it not at home, within our family and friendship structures where our children should feel the most safe in testing out the in and outs of accomplishments? Is it not these testings that will allow them to learn from their mistakes and their triumphs ~ so that as they grow, find these same tasks applicable to other areas in life, and in the world that they are better able to handle the situations before them? And handle the twists and turns possibly, better and with less strife simply because they have had time and time again to practice these very strategies, rather than waiting until "we" feel that they are deemed "old enough" or "strong enough" or "wise enough" or "careful enough or "responsible enough"? How else will our children learn if they do not learn by *doing and experiencing*? How else will they learn to be responsible if we do not give them opportunities to exhibit responsibility?

Another point to ponder would also be that of who is to say when a child is "ready" to learn a new concept or to take on something new? What is considered to be "age appropriate" for one child can be something totally imbalanced for another. One six year old may be quite adept at this age to cook grilled cheese sandwiches, while another is not even interested in looking at the stove.

Cooking

Speaking of cooking, one such way that our children's independence has grown and given them the willingness to go out on a limb and attempt and accomplish in most cases something that our children may not have ever tried before is in that of cooking.

For over a year now, our middle son Matthew 8, has grown to love cooking. I might add that he is quite the excellent chef! He loves to cook things like scrambled eggs and grilled cheese all on his own. Of course, I am or my husband is, always near by in case he needs assistance with the stove. We also have gone over the safety procedures for using appliances and first aid in the event of a burn etc. However, what I do not do, is I do not stand over him and watch his every move and tell him how he cannot do it or that I should do it for him. He only asks for mine or my husband's help if he needs it and we then help him not by doing it for him, but rather brainstorming with him ideas on how to approach the given situation and then allowing him the space in order for him to choose which direction he wishes to go. Unless he truly asks for us to do something for him, we allow him the freedom to explore.

For example, one time when Matthew was looking to cook all of us eggs for breakfast one morning, he had to choose how many eggs he would have to cook and if they would all fit into the pan he had brought out. When he asked me for help, I then suggested to him that he might want to ask how many each person wanted. When he did so, he discovered that he would need to make twelve eggs, which he determined to be a dozen. With math skills in hand, he then looked over at the small pan on the stove and without me having to say a word, utilizing deductive reasoning, realized that the pan would be just too small to fit the whole dozen eggs he was needing to cook. He therefore, while sounding so cute muttering to himself the contents of his newfound revelation, went into the cupboard and got the large pan out and happily started singing as he placed it on the burner and the proceeded to crack the eggs into the bowl.

My thoughts were of such pride and of such love for my son, as I watched him for I knew without a doubt that he was quite capable of handling the task at hand. I guess those are what I like to call as a "Mommy Moment".

I have to say how much it saddens me when I have watched parents time and time again as similar scenarios like this unfold with their own children, only to find that when the child asks for assistance, does the parent immediately take the pan out of the child's hand and say "Oh forget it! I will just cook them myself!" How sad it is to see that, how sad for the child, who's spirit looks like it was just trampled on, and I just shake my head in disbelief. I mean honestly, so what if the eggs would have spilled all over the floor? So what if the eggs would have turned out burnt? (Which they did not by the way, honestly, Matthew makes better eggs than I do!) So what if there is a mess that needs to be cleaned up? And guess what? There always is, whether it is us that is cooking or if our children are, and what do we do then?..... We clean it up!

This gives an opportunity to talk about and put into action (which is not a hard fast rule, but just a nice way) how to take care our kitchen and also so as not to leave the mess for someone else to clean. How when you cook that it is always a good idea to clean up either as you go or right after. This shows personal responsibility, cleanliness, and compassion. Life building skills and practical skills, such as logical thinking, deductive reasoning, and basic math are also applied here. It goes to show exactly how much you can truly learn while doing the simple act of cooking. This then is our purpose in life is to help in anyway we can to ascend our child's grow and ascend their spirits in the process!

The "Discovery Faerie"

In our home we believe in Faeries. There are Tree/Plant Faeries, the Tooth Faerie, and many other Faeries whom watch over us much as angels do. Also in our home, we embrace and celebrate all holidays from as many heritages as we can. Our children love learning about and in some cases adopting many of the customs and traditions of different heritages. So naturally during the holidays, we also have the Hanukkah Faerie who comes to visit our boys and leaves small Hanukkah treasures for each of the 8 nights.

Within that same spirit, is a faerie that also embrace in our home, that we call the Discovery Faerie. She is the Faerie who comes around our home and sprinkles her faerie dust or rather; she leaves materials that might be of interest around our home for our children to discover. She does this in such a way to provide a doorway to a path of discovery, to bring to light ways of learning that our children may not know of otherwise. It could be something as simple as sprinkling the faerie dust of magnets, blocks, geoboards, or books to read. Or it could be a whiteboard with some dry erase markers, or colored pencils and papers. Paper clips, a science experiment kit, or a new computer learning game. Anything that can be of use in discovery, the Discovery Faerie sprinkles around our home.

Another way the Discovery Faerie sprinkles her faerie dust magic involves taking the children out around town with the idea that utilizing our five senses to observe things they might not have come upon otherwise and that you are not able to sprinkle about the house. In our home, we call these FO's ~ "Faerie Outings"!

Sometimes such a "Faerie Outing" is as simple as driving a different route to the same old place, or going to a new grocery store rather than the usual one you go to. Or just getting in the car and driving, wherever it may lead us. If we something that we wish to stop and explore, then we do. Other successful outings could be that of construction sites, flea markets, outdoor concerts, or a museum.

Speaking of the museum, one of our favorite things that we love to do is go to the museums here in town. Every Tuesday, there is free museum day at our local museums. Usually two at least are free and rotate each week so that if you go every Tuesday of the month, you are able to enjoy all of them for free. All it costs is the gas *GEE* (money) to get down there. These museums cover such places as the Natural History Museum, The Fleet Science of Discovery Museum, the Japanese Friendship Gardens and more!

The "Faerie Outing" Budget

One of the questions that inevitable is raised when I do seminars on Life Long Learning is ~ Aren't "Faerie Outings" expensive? What about my budget, I do not have a lot of money to spend? Well, no FO's need not be expensive. It can be as inexpensive or as expensive as you choose it to be. One need not go very far to learn so much of what life has to offer you. All it takes is a bit of ingenuity and creativity to accomplish much on a small budget. As I mentioned earlier that construction sites are wonderful places to learn. With our every increasing population, housing tracts these days are being built *all* over the place these days. When you visit sometimes the construction workers will even show you around and demonstrate for you how things work and what goes where. Or you can visit during after-hour times and get your own "inside" view. And you can visit at various times to see the different stages of construction as well.

Another favorite fun thing that the boys and I love to do is that of "borrowing the bookstore". We all know what a wonderful resource the library can be, and I am all for the library. However, for our boys at least ~ and maybe you will find this with your children as well, especially if they had ever been within the schooling environment ~ our boys find the library to have many outdated books and it also tends to remind them too much of the horrors of their schooling experiences. Therefore, we borrow the bookstore instead. Many places nowadays, such as, Border's Books, Barnes & Noble Bookstores, and others, have special sections set aside or chairs and benches in designated areas for reading. The actually advocate you coming in and grabbing a book off the shelves and reading it! If you choose then to buy it, great, if not, then that is ok too! It is a wonderful way to read books and yet not have to spend the money to buy them. All of these examples are ways in which we can spend time together learning, coming away with shared experiences and conversations about those shared experiences. A lifetime of learning.

Love Affair with Learning

One of the most exciting aspects of Life Long Leaning is that of watching your children grow and learn through their passions in life. At times these passions can be quite intense, and other times they are often fleeting.

No, I am not describing a passionate romance between two people, but rather a "love affair" of learning in a particular thing that interests them. This is something can lead to a lifetime passion or maybe even become your child's life career. Or, it could be something that your child has an interest in for a day or two.

Some of the boys fleeting passions are that of making "experiments". Matthew particularly loves to do this. He will take odds and ends such as paperclips, bottle caps, string etc. and create concoctions. Some of these concoctions are like that of a triple magnifying glass or a pully using an old tape recorder. There is a wonderful book and video series called *"The Ultimate Book of Kid Concoctions", "The Ultimate Book of Kid Concoctions #2", "The Ultimate Book of Holiday Kid Concoctions", and the all new "Kid Concoctions & Contraptions"* by John E. Thomas & Danita Thomas which give hundreds of amazing concoctions that your child can create. They are available at http://www.kidconcoctions.com.

Right now, as I write this book, Yu-Gi-Oh is all three of our boys' passionate interest (http://entertainment.upperdeck.com/yugioh/en/). It is almost as if the eat, sleep, and breathe Yu-Gi-Oh. They go to Yu-Gi-Oh tournaments most weekends (two a weekend at times!); they trade cards, sell cards, duel it would almost seem like night and day. Their love of Yu-Gi-Oh has created an enormous opportunity for learning, as I go into much more detail in chapter nine.

Passions are not just limited to our children however. As I spoke of in chapter one of "contagious learning", an example of how our children do not only learn from us, but we learn from our children is in that of my husband, Aaron. Aaron has even come into his own passion with this love affair of Yu-Gi-Oh. This has been all due to the boys' passionate interest in it. Aaron has his own deck (decks actually!) and he and the boys immerse themselves in the world of Yu-Gi-Oh as often as the can for as long as they can.

"Contagious learning" has even come through me. As I am writing this book, my passion and interest for writing a book spurred on my on children's interests in writing their own books, illustrating them etc. Anthony recently wrote and illustrated his own book on why you should not watch so much T.V. in your lifetime. This came at a time when my husband Aaron was quite focused on watching that little black box, and Anthony had moved past the deschooling of the T.V. to find that there was more to life and more to learn then only watching TV to learn. It was rather cute how his book came out saying, "This is the T.V. You should not watch so much T.V. in your lifetime".

Matthew was six and a half at the time I started writing this book, when he began writing and illustrating his own monster deck like that of Yu-Gi-Oh cards. I have watched with pride as I have seen his deck go from only have his sketches on the cards to having the precise writing of how each card works and what it does. This is all from a boy whom in the schooling environment was silently told through he could not read or write and had to have a reading specialist "teach" him, that he was not smart enough on his own to learn. His beginning to write and love of writing would never have blossomed again, had it not been for me immersing myself into my own passion, my own interest.

Matthew, not too long ago described how he would hide in shame with his reading, trying to guess from the pictures what was in the books because he was being shamed for not being able to read the words, and that when the teachers found out that he could not read, they would tell him "Well, then you can only read from *those* book over *there*" in front of the class. While I harbor no ill feelings towards the teachers in his life, as they were only doing what they felt was the best they could do within the compulsory structure they had to deal with, as I too can understand that having had to have done this myself when I was teaching, I am so grateful that we were able to get Matthew out of that environment and to enable to him to be a Life Long Learner. His spirit has soared and he has grown so much from being able to learn on his own.

Anthony, since the day that he learned how to speak fluently at about the age of 15 months, has always said that he wants to be a Veterinarian. He has a passion for dogs in particular. When he was younger he would state that he was going to be a "Doggie Doctor". His collection of stuffed animal dogs is *so* large that there is really no room for himself on his bed when he sleeps at night! Part of his passion also involves caring for our three dogs ~ Sandi, Luckie, and Chip. He grooms them, walks them, bathes them, brushes their coats, and gives them herbal remedies when they are ill, the whole nine yards. He enjoys taking care of them, as he knows that these are all things he will need to learn and more if he does truly wish to take his life long passion and turn it into a career. Another way that Anthony cares for animals, and Matthew as well, is through the playing of computer and internet games. Two such games, *Dogs5* and *Neopets* offer wonderful virtual ways of learning how to care for and nurture animals. It is a digital format to learn such concepts as communication skills, record keeping, as well as real life experiences with animals.

Chris, his passion lies with computers. Anything computer related, he can do it. He has had this passion since he got his first computer at the age of four. For the last nine plus year now, he has been tinkering with, taking apart, and learning all about the world of computers. He knows how to design websites, repair, networking, troubleshooting of PC's and more. Anytime my computer is not working or the network is down, I call "Chris" and boy he is right there! And of course, he looks at me like I am nuts and says "Oh mom, this is all you have to do is this ......" and on and on he will go about how whatever is not working with the computer needs to be fixed in computer language, which of course I have *no* clue what he is talking about! As of right now, Chris has been working on a flyer, website, and computer set up so that he can start up his own PC supply and repair business. This has its' potential to turn into a career passion of his.

Now, of course, our boys have their share of ever fleeting love affairs with certain passionate interests. There is the remote control cars, of which they love playing with and troubleshooting when they break, but once they are broken beyond foreseeable repair, they move on to the next interest. There has been interests in rocks, paper mache, candle making, writing on the white board in our bedroom (and sometimes they will even write math problems along with their sketches and stories they make on the board), sewing, guitar playing and many, many other interests. Much more than I can ever write here!

One of the most wonderful parts of Life Long Learning is that we simply have our whole lives to learn from as in-depth of an interest as we wish, as well as the fleeting interests. The key is to get into our children's' passions with them and learn together. It can open up the world to so many other connections of learning that you never even dreamed possible! Joyce Fetteroll so eloquently stated when she spoke at the 2002 Live and Learn Conference in Boston, Massachusetts, *"Think in terms of creating an atmosphere of wonder where people are genuinely curious about life and where there are intriguing things to be curious about. Not because that's what would be good for them, but as a gift to them with no strings attached. Think in terms of their interests leading them out to the world rather than looking for pathways for the world to get into them."*

Multiple Siblings with a Variety of Interests.....
Oh Whatsoever Shall We Do?

Oh! Whatsoever shall we do when we have multiple children, all of whom have unique and separate interests from that of our other children! I suppose that I feel that I am one of the lucky ones in life to where this is not as much of an issue here in our home. Our boys have this cohesiveness about them in that of not being limited by age or gender constraints, have adopted pretty much the same interests. Chris, being almost 14, still loves Yu-Gi-Oh and Pokemon, and Matthew loves tinkering with Chris on the computer and learning what he wishes to learn from Chris. Anthony loves to play a computer game called "Dogs 5" and as does Matthew.

I am glad for this because there is a freedom to explore, be passionate about, and interested in a wide variety of things in life, without the stereotypical responses that are given by same aged peers in the schooling environment, such as, "Ew! You still like *THAT*!" or "Pokemon is for babies!" and the like.

That said, there are still times, that one or more of our boys will have an interest in something that the other or others do not. In cases such as this, there are many methods we try on to smooth out the kinks, so to speak.

An example of this is was one time when we all wished to go to eat somewhere and Anthony wanted to eat at home. In this case, we were able to talk with Anthony to find that he did indeed want to go to bond with us, but that he just did not want to eat from that particular restaurant. Thus, at his request, we made him something to eat at home first before going.

There have been times when Matthew and Anthony wish to go to the park, and Chris does not wish to go. Therefore, since Chris is old enough to be at home by himself, he has said that he would stay home while I take Matthew and Anthony to the park. Another way we have approached things is sort of like that of teams. If a few of us wish to do something and the rest do not, I will take the ones who wish to go, and my husband will stay home with whomever does not wish to go, or vice versa. Or if Chris wants to do something or go somewhere where Matthew and Anthony do not wish to, then either my husband or I will take Chris. We also do our best to make arrangements to go or do whatever that is at a time when one of us will be home to stay with Matthew and Anthony, and the other take Chris.

There are times, though, that inevitably, my husband will be at work, and one of our boys will want to go somewhere and the others will not. If that person happens to be Matthew or Anthony, then Chris is, more often then not, ok with staying home and watching the other of the two of them, while I take whichever the one who wishes to go or do something to that place or event etc. If it is not, and it is Chris whom wishes to, then what we usually do in this case is that I explain to Matthew and Anthony that this is something special that Chris wishes to do, and that I will spend time with each of them later that day or evening, doing something that they wish to do. More often than not, this is alright with them.

Separate Interests on the Homefront

When it comes to separate interests when we are at home, our boys often again have this cohesiveness about them that they just seem to blend together and the apart as they need to. They each know each other so well, that they are able to know intrinsically when they need a break from being together and when one or more of them needs the space in order to pursue an interest that they may or may not all share. In that respect, I do not have to "do" anything, this is just happens on it's own, and really comes from a sense of them each really knowing and getting to know one another on a day to day basis.

When it comes to multiple interests between multiple siblings and sharing that with them, the key here is balance. Balance in the fact that if there is an interest that one child wishes to share with Mom and so does the other child, that a balance can be found. The way we have done this is for one child to know, "Ok, mom or dad is going to spend x amount of time with your brother/sister learning and sharing what he/she wants to do, and then when I am done, then it will be your turn".

This seems to work well with children whom are able to grasp the concept of waiting and that of waiting their turn. For those children whom do not, a shorter period of time is usually the best approach, as is using things like an egg timer, so that the child knows that when the timer goes off, that it will be their turn. Or if they are watching a TV program, letting them know that you will spend time with their brother or sister until the show is over is helpful as well.

Invariably, what tends to happen, at least here on our homefront, is that upon spending time with one of our boys with whatever their interest is at that given moment that they wish to share, the other boys wish to come in and see what is going on and it turns into learning for everyone, thus all or most of each person's separate interests become in some part and on some level, all of our interests.

This occurred one time when Matthew had learned how to make a streamline video singing "Happy Birthday" to Anthony on his computer. This was originally something that Matthew was pursuing as an interest of his own. He had discovered the software on a CD he had gotten for his digital camera and learned how to do this video making all on his own. However, upon gifting this computer video to his brother via email for his birthday, Anthony asked Matthew if he could show him how he did it. As a result, they spent the next 3 hours in Matthew's room on his computer, making their own streamline computer videos together.

I have seen within my own family and through other families who also use this Life Long Learning philosophy, how being inclusive in this manner and modeling it helps to provide that cohesiveness to where there is not such a struggle over who is going to get time to pursue what interest with whom. It is not that these interests are forced upon the other children, for if they choose not to be involved upon viewing what is happening, they can choose to be or not to be.

However, I feel simply stating to a child "This is your sister/brothers time, and you are not allowed to be involved" does nothing more than beget the problem and turns what is meant to be a pleasant time of discovery and learning, into a tantrum and screaming match. It does so, because it goes back to the old saying that if mom and dad say it is forbidden, I am going to want to do it just because they say it is forbidden. Thus, it then becomes a tantrum with the other child over why he/she cannot be included and thus making mom or dad or both and the child upset, and the other child then looses out on the quality time they wanted to begin with.

So, while our wish is to give the undivided attention to the child whom is looking for this in sharing their interest or passion with you, at the same time, we should leave the door open for any and all whom are interested to feel free to explore with us. Indeed, if this freedom is given, then most of the time, they may come and take a peek, looking for a minute or two to see what their brother or sister is into with you, and then simply chooses to do something else while you are with your other child. This then gives the child whom is seeking that one on one interaction the freedom to share with you and with others if they so choose to, without feeling the confines of those around them hoarding over them just waiting until they are done so that they can spend time with mom or dad.

It also gives children the freedom of expression and a wanting to share with others of their gifts and talents, while still knowing that whatever their passion and interest is can be their passion or interest but it can be shared without fear of it somehow being taken away if more than one person wishes to explore it with them.

Many times Anthony does this, as when Matthew is sharing something, like his sketches that he is working on. One day Anthony simply came over and sat for a few minutes with us, and then went off and imagination role-played with what he calls his "guys" (his figurines of many types he plays with). Another day, he will want to grab his sketchpad or clipboard and sketch with Matthew and I. Another time, when all of us were sketching it turned into a whole art lesson on how to draw different Pokemon characters, as we found several websites with how to steps to sketch out several Pokemon characters. We also have done this using a few how to books, such as, "How to Draw Sea Life Creatures", and "How to Draw Insects".

For children whom are that of a baby or toddler, this multiple sibling, multiple interests, can be that of a challenge. I know that when Matthew and Anthony were small, being only seventeen months apart and that they were five and a half to seven years apart from Chris respectively, that this was an interesting quest indeed. Many a times you find that the younger children tend get more of the hands on day-to-day guidance of things like diaper changing and toilet training, as well as the sharing of interests. Whereas your older children, though they may need and want to be with you just as much, it is in another capacity. Juggling this can be a challenge, but the key is always balance. Balance in whatever way works for you and your family. And respect. Respecting each child for who they are and what they are here to give.

~

You can be upset because rosebushes have thorns,
Or you can rejoice because thorn bushes have roses.
~ Unknown

Chapter Five

Cinderella…..Cinderella……
Life Long Learning ~ Chores and Rewards

One of the biggest debates with Life Long Learning is that of the topic of Chores. I have come to find that not having a list of chores seems to work best. We do not have a "set chores" list or that they even **have to** do chores. And we do not have a reward system for doing chores either. The way we get cleaning done in our home seems to happen something like this ~ I will be cleaning for example say the living room, and then through the natural progression of things, one or more of the boys will come in and ask "Hey Mom what are you doing?" and they will pitch in on their own, ask me what I need help with or just start cleaning on their own.

I must say that I have never been one who has believed in "forcing" children to do chores. The common thought among some parents is that if you "train your children right" while they are growing, then they will become these wonderful helpful spouses and parents when they have children of their own. I deem that quite the contrary is true. I infer that the reason why most boys grow to be men who are not the helpful husbands and dads that their wives wish they were is due to the fact that they were "forced" to do chores when they were younger. I also feel that this too is why husbands the majority of the time do not help or want to help their wives with the "housework", or "chores" as, the husbands so lovingly call it, when their wives ask them or nag at them, because they were "nagged" and "forced" by their parents to "perform" by having to do chores. I have come to find that none of us like to be forced to do something they do not wish to do, no matter what it is.

Have you ever noticed the difference when you are cleaning the house and your husband comes in and asks "Is there anything I can do to help?" or "Here, let me do that for you" ~ that is choice and then there is a willingness to help, whereas the non-willingness to help when he has been nagged 50 bazillion times to clean the yard. I also feel that this is why girls grow into women whom spend their lives being really proficient in taking care of everyone else and everyone else's needs but rarely if ever take care of themselves and their needs. Then they become mothers whom are tired, weary, and eventually resentful over the years of the fact that they must take care of all of the housework themselves, when they have husbands, as I have described above, that do not help.

Now you may feel these beliefs may sound like very stereotypical judgments. In fact they are not judgments at all, but rather merely observations that I have surmised from countless discussions with men and women of all walks of life, of individuals that I have spoken to and have observed. Nor is my reasoning stereotypical in nature, as not every single parent on this earth has these types of tendencies. In fact, there are many spouses and parents whom are helpful to their spouses free from the constraints of their upbringing. However, in general terms, these are the things of which I have seen over the years as both a parent, a counselor, as a teacher in the schooling environment, and now as a Life Long Learner, that has given me cause to formulate these beliefs.

Let's think for a moment about cleaning from a child's perspective. Children are a lot smarter than we tend to give them credit for. If the house seems disastrous, then no child would just dive in and clean up all by themselves without any help. It would seem impossible to a child, that if mom and dad are overwhelmed by having to clean a mess up all by themselves, and are not sure where to start cleaning and cannot imagine when the end will be near, when it will all be clean again, then why would a child put him or herself through that? If we are overwhelmed then how can we expect them to remain composed and clean all by themselves?

Now, I must say that there are exceptions to this. Anthony for one is just this exception. There are times when he will go in and clean a whole room of the house, whether it be that of his own room or another room, completely without so much as thought. So while I know that there are exceptions, as a societal generality, it is not what would be seen as the "norm".

If you were to look at this from yet another perspective ~ is cleaning together, as a group, not what the civilizations of long ago did? Did they not work together as a unit? In a tribe, everyone helped out, hand in hand to get whatever needed to be done, done. No one sat the children down and said "Ok Matthew, you *have* to do your chores, here they are, and if you do them, then we will have a treat when you are done and if not you are grounded"! There were no such things as "chores" in the civilizations of long ago....everyone simply worked together. With the exception of the time in history where there were slaves, the life of the average family in civilizations of long ago was one in which assisting with the daily happenings was just a part of everyday life as a family unit ~ a natural giving and helping home environment where things were done together on a constant basis, so that taking care of their homes was something that was not a set of forced chores, but simply just a way of blending together as part of life. It was seen as a joyful part of life, not a dreaded one.

As someone on a discussion list I belonged to once so perfectly wrote:

"Think about how you would want a friend to ask for your help fixing a car or doing something you did not really enjoy. You could probably think of dozens of other things you would rather do with your time. And that is something your friend should realize and appreciate. So how could your friend ask for help? How should she treat you while you helped? How should she treat you after, to acknowledge that she really appreciated you giving her some of your valuable time to do something she knew you really did not want to do? What if she asked you to keep her company and you spent a couple hours of pleasant conversation? What if she asked for you to hand her things and hold things while she worked? What if when you made a mistake or did not do something the way she wanted it done, she apologized for asking you to do something that was not as easy or interesting for you as she thought it would be? What if she thanked you sincerely when she was done? And then invited you in for some tea and conversation or let you return to what you wanted to do or whatever she felt she could do as a sign of her appreciation? Would you feel like helping her again if she asked? Now turn that around. What if you had another friend who demanded that you help her work on her car? You are her friend and you have certain responsibilities. And what if you could not help to her standards and she got angry with you when you failed? What if you really hated working on cars and wanted it over and done? And you felt like doing as little as possible so you could get out of there sooner? What if when she was done she was angry with you and said "You should be helping more and I should not even need to ask." Which friend

*would you be likely to help next time? Which friend is building a
relationship with you and which is tearing it down?"*

Joy, Oh Joy!

Now this is not to say that I never ask our children for help around the
house, as I do at times. I am just not demanding or expecting that
they have to do so. On occasion, I have been known to ask our
children to help me out by taking care of the unloading and loading of
the dishwasher while I am gone running an errand. I do this not as a
means of giving them a "chore" to do, but rather as request

However, if the dishwasher is not done when I come home, there is
no "punishment". I will gently ask again, and if it is not done later that
day, then I will usually take care of the task at hand. I do so, without
grumbling at the boys for not having done it, nor do I punish them for
it. I believe that it is due to this approach that it is rare that the boys
rarely not finish something that I have asked them for help with. I
believe that this comes from the fact that our children are always
given the choice of helping. It is from choice that we learn best, and in
given that choice, they feel happy then to give freely of themselves. In
doing so, they gain the self-satisfaction knowing that they have done
something to assist someone else of their own free will.

So it goes then that should they choose not to help, that I have come
to be ok with that as well. I have come to find joy and peace in
cleaning for my family whether they choose to help when I ask it of
them or not. Cleaning the house is like giving a gift to my family, a gift
that I know that if I give freely, without complaint, it will be appreciated
much more than if I grumble about giving it. We do not grumble, when
giving a gift to a friend, so why should we grumble when giving the gift
of caring for them?

I find that the *Life's Daily Joys* are here for a reason ~ for me to find
the joy, happiness, and love that I get from taking care of my family.
So scrubbing poop off of the toilets is not the most fun thing in the
world, but I have found that if you model taking care of your house
happily, even if it seems as if you do not ever make any real progress
or feel it's getting really clean, but if you look after things calmly and
happily, that your children will be more likely to participate in the
process. If you are grumping around growling about things being in a
state of chaos, how are they ever supposed to feel that they could
manage it? If you cannot handle it, how could they?

As this same person I spoke of above continued in their post on the discussion list.....

"...It is the same with the house. If you would appreciate help, you can ask, but you cannot expect it. You need to appreciate that you have imposed on someone else's time to help you with something that is your responsibility. Their bedrooms belong to them. They can keep them to their own standards. If the standards bother you, you can ask if they would not mind if you clean it. But your cleaning needs to be for *you*, not for them. Do not expect them to appreciate it. Do not expect them not to appreciate it, either! And do not expect them to maintain it. You are doing it for yourself. There should be no expectations on them. Expect *yourself* to appreciate having turned chaos into order. With that change in attitude will come a change in theirs. It will not be magical. If they have been coerced for years, they are going to think your new attitude is a new way of making them do what you want them to. But they will change if your change is about changing you, not about changing them. As for helping around the house, ask them to keep you company. Ask them to do you a favor and then express appreciation for them giving up something they would rather be doing in order to do something for you. Model how you would want them to ask you to interrupt something important that you are doing (even if they do not see it as important) to do them a favor. Model how you would want them to express appreciation for you going out of your way to help them out. "

One of my most endearing *"Mommy Moments"* for me came once when asking Chris if he would unload and reload the dishwasher. The next thing I knew, Chris was asking Matthew and then Matthew asked Anthony if they would help and before I knew it, all three of them were doing the dishwasher, laughing and having a great time doing it too! I was sitting in the living room at the time, reading, and all of the sudden I hear Chris say, "Ok Mom, you can have one of your sweet *"Mommy Moments"* now!" The act of kindness, of pure love, made me cry, and it really was a *Mommy Moment*.

Well, I know what you must be saying though. I know, I know, there are those of you whom may be resisting this, saying to yourselves "but, but.....I still **need** my children's help! I cannot possibly do all of this cleaning myself!" Well then, if there are still those times when you feel you still need help picking up their stuff or cleaning in general, make a game of it. Make it fun by putting on some music, blast it, and before you know it, you will be finished. You know just like in Snow White and the Seven Dwarfs, "*Just whistle while you work*".

I can recall Chris being about three years old and the only way he would ever help me clean anything was if I played the Barney "Clean Up" song. I used to have to play the tape and/or sing the song over and over! It made cleaning up together fun and less stressful. One mom I heard about wrote once that she used to have Lego Races with her children, trying to see which one of them could throw more bricks in the bucket, and who could do it loudest! Another thing you can do is to offer to let them feather-dust, rather than hogging all the fun for yourself. The likely hood of them helping us out from time to time is greater, because it will be a pleasant and fun experience, and the learning that comes from it is priceless.

The one thing I have come to learn is that as a Life Long Learning family, our home is **NEVER** spotlessly clean. Cleaning never comes before learning and fun in our home, so there are many a things that will wait until the next day to be done. And so that once something in the house does become "clean" the cycle starts all over again. Happily so. Our home may never be spotless, but it is never on the verge of being condemned, either! In the grand scheme of things, does it really matter so much whether our houses are spotless or not? Will the world come to an end if the dishes do not get cleaned or the living room straightened up right this second? The world and all of us in it will still be here and the mess will still be there if it gets clean right that second or a few hours later.

You know, another thing that I have learned over the years is that you do not get another chance to be a parent to your children right now, today. When they are grown and are on their own, you can have the cleanest house in the neighborhood. But what is the most important thing today? What will you be happier remembering in your old age that your house always looked nice or that your children had fun loving times with you, were learning and happy? What will your children be happy to remember about their time with you? Dirty houses always wait for you to get around to them. Loving and learning with your children should not have to.

Rewards

One thing that I have come to find in Life Long Learning is that reward systems for children just simply do not work. All that children come to learn from reward systems is how to get good at getting the reward, not changing their behavior. Sure maybe you got them to get the chore done, or they were good for whatever length of time you ask them to, **BUT** if you ask them two weeks from that chore or being good what information they learned, they will not be able to tell you. Or the next time you want that chore done, you will not be able to simply ask, you will have to offer yet another reward to ensure it gets done, therefore perpetuating the cycle. The child only learns that the object is for them to get the reward, not learning the value of doing what was asked of them, that "chore" or the value of knowing that they are be of assistance to be a productive, helpful loving member of the family. All they know is the reward; they do not see the other values. Their eye is always "on the prize", rather than that of the life lessons to be learned and the bliss in the heart that comes from assisting another.

This is why I do not believe that rewards work. I want my children to learn that life has its' own rewards, not that of material rewards for good deeds done, but rather the inner rewards that life has to offer us. I want our children to know the value of what the lesson is to be learned, of what it is to help out together as a family. Of the satisfaction and warm feeling that come from knowing that they helped someone, of doing good deeds for others, and doing a job well done comes from within. You know, that warm fuzzy feeling you feel inside rather than getting some external reward for helping out or doing a good deed or a job well done.

This is what I believe will one day lead our children to be the helpful, loving, and caring husbands, fathers, and productive members of society that I know they will be. Not because they received some sticker or some other type of reward, but because the reward came from within, from life and all of the many joys and miracles there are in it. Choice always opens doors ~ force, bribing, or offering rewards to get children to do whatever it is you want them to do, do not.

~

Children will not remember you for the material things you provided, but for the feeling that you cherished them ~ Richard L. Evans

Chapter Six

Green Energy Exchange

I am often asked by other mom's and other homelearning families, "What do your children do for allowance?" I have to admit that when my children were younger and in the schooling environment, they often would have a case of the "gimmes" and "I wants". We could not go through a store of any kind ~ grocery, department store etc. without one, both, or all three of the boys asking for something. Our children also seemed to during this time period of being in school, had this affinity to "stuff". They seemed to have a hard time letting go of things.

We also over the years, when each one of the boys were in school, had gone through the times where we would set up the old list of "chores" or things they could do to earn an allowance once a week, only when they had asked to do so. This usually came from peer pressure from schooling friends who were able to buy the bigger, better, and more "in" items and they did not want to feel left out. The allowance issue in that manner never seemed to last long in our home, simply because it was driven by a "schooled" mentality that was reinforcing a materialistic view of the world in order to fit in. Once our boys realized this on their own, without my husband, nor myself, having to point it out, the allowance issue became a non-issue.

The term "allowance" to me seems to be very degrading to children if you really look at the word closely. I mean, would we simply "allow" others to pay us for all of the love and energy that you place into your efforts? By all implications we are saying just that to our children. We are say that we will "allow" you to do some "chore" or "some thing" and then we "allow" you to get money for it, when we say, with our permission. When we go out into the workforce ourselves or develop our own business, as society works at this time, it is the natural progression of life that we will receive monetary compensation for our efforts in life, our service to others. Therefore, we have not been "allowed" as if we have to ask permission to do this. Therefore, the term allowance is really are rather degrading way to place so little value upon our children.

There will be times when the boys will be saving up for something, or just saving money in general, and we will be asked by our children what "jobs" they can do, like daddy does when he goes to work. As Anthony, so poignantly will ask "How much money will I get paid to cleaning....whatever it is (the garage, the family room, the dishwasher, the laundry etc.), just like daddy gets paid when he works?" These questions sparked by Anthony's interest in finding a way to receive monetary compensation, then opened the doorway with all of our boys for learning about the true intention of money in life as it has become in our society.

Money is energy. Money is a manifesting energy. An exchange of this money occurs when energy is expended upon a task, as a form of transference of energy ~ energy expended upon a task, thus money given in exchange. I believe therefore, that as Life Long Learners, we should consider the money that our children obtain for their effort in life as a gift of love, as all people should, rather than seeing money as just a way to accumulate material wealth. Therefore, rather than our children just simply "earning money" in life, we can term it as *GEE* (pronounced as the letter G) *"Green Energy Exchange"*.

Green Energy Exchange

When I tell people, children especially about *GEE,* I sometimes get the funny saying like *"GEE* that is great!" or the children especially like the term to think of it in money terms as far as how many "G's" (grand for $1,000) they could have. Or the children deem as more self actualized see the term *GEE* as something like Jackie Chan's uncle in the show "Jackie Chan Adventures" when he says "Uncle need Chi spell" *GEE* sounding much like Chi. So it catches on and is an easy concept to bring for into our Life Long Learning way of life.

Learning the concepts and harnessing the power that *GEE* has and the utilization of these powers and principles of *GEE*, I must say, has been, and continues to be, a wonderful Life Long Learning lesson for our children. Before, when the boys were in school, they had what I would call that "schooled-like mentality". Anytime we went to a place like Chuck E. Cheese, they would automatically be raving lunatics, (being so happy to be "free" from school) wanting more and more *GEE* to spend, getting their tickets, and then wanting to spend them "right now" on the junk they have there.

As a result of being a Life Long Learning family, some very miraculous things have occurred with regard to *GEE*. Now a sense of calmness has come about our boys with regard to *GEE*. While our children recognize that *GEE* is something that we have in our society at this time that is a means to provide us with the things in life that are needed ~ food, clothing, shelter etc. they have also come to embrace *GEE* on a learning level that not many children are enabled to do so by their parents. They have embraced it for the energy exchange that it brings rather than how much they can accumulate for "material wealth" or "things".

So that when we go to a place like Chuck E. Cheese or any place that has video games, they actually do not beg us fifty million times for *GEE,* nor do they spend all of their tickets on what I would consider junk, as they have too come to see some of the items that are there are junk. The last time we went, **all** of them informed me (separately, away from their brothers) that they wished to save their tickets for the next time we came. We walked out without a single toy!

We are also able to go into a store like Michael's, for instance, during the holidays, when all of the holiday decorations are out and when every other child has the "gimmies" and the "I wants", in terms of having the most decorations out on their lawns, our children walk through and actually enjoy admiring and appreciating all of the beautiful items in the store knowing that while that might wish to have them, that they are not attached to those items **so** much that they just have to have them right that second.

I remember this past holiday season when our boys had gotten holiday gift cards from our relatives that they wanted to go to Toys-R-US to purchase items using their gift cards. I can remember beaming with pride as I watched Matthew buy only two packages of Yu-Gi-Oh cards ($8 worth of *GEE*) and save the remaining 17 *GEE's* ($17) for as he put it "another time, mom, I will buy something more with it later. I do not need to spend all of my *GEE* now, just because I just got it".

Generous Spirit

One of the other wonderful Life Long Learning moments, in which our children learned of the generosity of others, and in that which you give will come back to you ten fold, came from a most unlikely source. Just as our children can learn much from us so too we can learn much from our children.

Chris had been looking on the computer at a Yu-Gi-Oh card that he has been wanting and did not have the *GEE* to buy it. Anthony, upon noticing this, took it upon himself to go downstairs and said, "Daddy, can you pay for the shipping, and I will give you the last $3.59 of the *GEE* I have left that Poppie and Grandma gave me for Christmas, so that I can get the Yu-Gi-Oh card for Chris for Christmas?" It turned out that the card was only $3.50, so when Anthony heard that, he said "Yippee! I have nine cents left, Daddy I will give it you to help pay for the shipping!" :)

His generous spirit and him giving of his last little bit of *GEE* he had left to make his brother's Christmas brighter, made me feel so filled with love and made me so proud that he is my son. The fact that he was so happy with the fact that he only had nine cents left, that he had such joy over having that nine cents left made my heart overfill with such love. Then in giving that last nine cents of *GEE* that he had left to help with the shipping, just made me cry with joy and love.

Bless my Anthony for showing us all that this is what the holidays are all about no matter which way one celebrates them. That it is not about *GEE*, but about the love and joy we give to others, even if it means that we have nothing left ourselves that we can and should be ok with that. That it is not just at the holidays we should be giving of ourselves, of our love and of our talents to help others in need, but everyday.

I know completely in my heart and my soul that his generous spirit and gift of love will be returned to him ten fold. It was a Life Long Learning "Mommy Moment" gift from the smallest of my children, I shall not ever forget. As they say, good things come in small packages.

"Stuff"

It seems that as a Life Long Learning family, as any family does, you accumulate a lot of "stuff". Being that we are Life Long Learners, this seems to be more so than that of other families simply due to the fact that our learning accumulations are everywhere. And not just in the home either, our learning items seem to extend to the car, friends, relatives, and neighbors homes and so on.... I mean let's face it, we all have a lot of "stuff". We all feel there are things that we state "Oh, I might need that someday" or "I am keeping this for when we are doing to do this project or that project". Before we know it, our "stuff" has taken over our homes and our lives.

While there are possessions which are within our home, that we still hold dear, over the last couple of years, our family has found it much easier to let go of the "things" that we really do not need or do not have a use for anymore. We have come to view our love, our family, the love that we have for others, and the love we share with others as worth more than our material wealth.

Moving to a smaller home this past year has made the process of clean out the clutter a bit easier to handle. I think moving is a wonderful Life Long Learning tool ~ a kind of like a way for life to somewhat give you that little kick in the butt to do that which you might not do otherwise.

It is funny because in the children's earlier years, we moved every year to year and a half along side my husband's then chosen career. We always used to loath it. The teacher in me used to rationalize me keeping all of this "stuff", thinking that, "Oh, one day, I will have a use for this kind of a thing".

We have come to embrace moving, as it is a time of renewal ~ a time of releasing the old, to creating space for the new energy to enter into our lives. Cleaning out the house and garage during our move, we came to see all of the "stuff" that we had been holding onto and for what? If someone else may have a use for the very thing that we are hanging onto, then what right do we have to hold onto it if we are not using it or no longer need it? Why should we be selfish and keep it? What do we have to gain in keeping that of which someone can use? Should we not be sharing that of what we do not need with another who is in need?

I find that excess "stuff" in the house that is unused or is not stored for any particular purpose is just excess draining energy that need not be there. Keeping "stuff" we do not need right at that moment or in the immediate future is just a way for us holding excess energy onto and into something. We spend so much time placing that energy upon those "things" we are not utilizing, when that that energy can be used more effectively towards creating in the now. If that item is really something that we truly need, by letting go of it in the now, if it is truly needed again in the future, that very thing or something like it or better than it, will then come into our lives when it is needed.

In evaluating whether to get rid of or keep something, I invite you to consider these questions: Do I really love it? Do I really need it? If I do need it, what is my time frame for using it? How do I feel when I think of this item? Do I really want to have to store, clean, care for, and think about this item? Can I do without this item very easily?

Getting rid of excess "stuff" by having a garage sale is one way to release our stuff. Yet the best way to release one's "stuff" is simply to give it away. Find a friend, relative, or someone you know who you feel will receive the greatest joy from those items, and give it to them. Or I invite you to take it yourself to a nearby Salvation Army, Goodwill, or American Red Cross center. I say physically transport the items yourself, rather than having someone else come pick them up, so as to give yourself the experience of the release.

As they say, "One person's junk, is another person's treasure". All we have is now, so why wait to hang onto things to use it someday? The thing of it is that all of our possessions are truly not ours anyhow. If we really stop to think about it, in the grand scheme of things, we are only here upon the planet for a certain length of time. In that time, we are merely "borrowing" if you will what resources, items, and yes "things" that we need to utilize upon our journey. As they say, you cannot take all your possessions with you when you go. So, why do we have such an attachment to that of what is truly not ours, that is only being borrowed while we are here on this earth? We do not truly have something until we know in our hearts that it is not really ours to begin with, this it is something that we borrow while we are here on this earth. Only then can we feel free truly to give it away.

As a family this past holiday season, each one of us, went through the rest of our "stuff" from the move, and we took three loads over to our local Goodwill center. It felt so good to know that we were not only getting rid of that excess energy that was no longer needed in our lives, but we were giving to others who will have a need for it. There are so many people in this world who have so much less than we have, and if we are able to make someone else's face light up when they see that item that we have to give, then *that* is what truly matters. It was the best holiday present I gave to myself and to another this past year and is something I look forward to doing not just at the holidays, but all life long.

Organizing the "Stuff" We Use

All of us have that "stuff" that we use everyday or occasionally anyhow. One of the best ways to organize that "stuff" that we need and use daily is something I started doing about 5 years ago now. One January morning, when "*A HOG*" (After Holiday Organizational Bug) hit me, I went to my local department store and bought about 45 or so storage boxes, clear ones, and opaque ones. The opaque boxes

I stored all of the holiday decorations that I knew that I would not have to see through the boxes until the following year, and the clear ones for things we use regularly such as tools, children project stuff, wrapping ribbons etc.

The boys all pitched in and in no time, our house became CF ~ Clutter Free. Even now, most of our "stuff" is in some form of storage tub. Most of them are see through and put in the cupboards so we can easily find things. I also have some things in wicker baskets, such as, pens and such on our kitchen counter and baskets for the children's toys etc. The house still gets cluttered and although it is never spotless, it does make our "stuff" more manageable. I guess you can call it OC ~ Organized Chaos!

Eliminating what we truly do not need has opened the door for us to be more comfortable in our smaller home, and live more simply. Not having so much "stuff" has also meant less to clean and care for, which means more time for what is really important in life ~ being together and loving each other.

Entrepreneurs

Our boys being able to handle their own *GEE* from an early age is also a key Life Long Learning lesson that we have come to know. Our boys have become very adept to finding other avenues to have *GEE* manifest into their lives. Life Long Learning lends itself to ingenuity. When free from the constraints of the "have to's" and "must's" of compulsory education, our children's minds are able to open up to any and all possibilities for creation of anything that they desire to manifest in their lives.

It is in that spirit of ultimate possibility that our boys have become entrepreneurs in many ways, a learning that will go with them in life wherever they go. They have done things such as their own garage sales, to trading of items that they have or bartering of their talents in exchange for something that they may need or desire. They have, in discovering *Ebay* (as I will write in more detail later in chapter eight) have sold items of theirs and have even gone so far as to purchase items directly for lesser value and then resell them for higher value then that of what they purchased it for.

Anthony, at six, started making his own *"Pokemon Card Sale"* signs and would sell his cards out at our community park that we have across the street from our home. He always looks so darn cute dragging his table and chair outside and asking me "Mommy, where is the tape?" or "Did I spell my sign right?" One time he made $7.00!

Our oldest son, Chris, at almost 14 has been working on plans to have his own website design/computer repair business. He has been developing his own site, been involved in the process of purchasing the phone line, and is currently developing his own fliers for distribution. He is also working on another possible business venture in that of his own computer store as he says "that is like Fry's!"

All three boys have developed a knack for beading necklaces. A girlfriend of mine and I started a beading business, and it has blossomed into a small family side business. It is an evolving Life Long Learning process that is enabling them to see exactly how a business is built and run from the ground up. Chris has utilized is talents in his eye for design and symmetry, beading necklaces of many different styles and intricate patterns. He has his own bead box, and as we market and sell them together, he will receive profits from his beautiful pieces of artistry. He has already helped me do so at swap meets, and getting ready for a local bazaar. All of the boys being involved in every aspect of the process, as they have expressed an interest to learn every step of the way.

Matthew too, has developed his own talents in that of making earrings. He too, has his own bead box with supplies that he chose out and helped to pay for to make earrings. As we sell our handcrafted jewelry, he will reap the profits of his efforts. Anthony, also has his own beading box, and enjoys making different patternings of necklaces and bracelets. He calls them his protection necklaces/bracelets.

Once the *GEE* comes to fruition for them in whatever form it is manifested, the boys have chosen to be in charge of what happens to the *GEE* that they accumulate. This for them as they see it means ~ that they are responsible for keeping it in a safe place, how much they will spend and how much they will save if they choose to. Through their Life Long Learning purchasing experiences, they have learned to how much taxes or shipping are on any given item and that it needs to be calculated in when they purchase something. They have also learned the value of knowing that when they have spent their *GEE* and it is all gone, that there is no more until they can devise another avenue for manifesting more. They also know too, that the manifesting more does not mean simply come and ask mom and dad and they will give it to you, as this is not always the case.

Now, I must say though, that we are by no means mean-spirited parents whom do not give our children any *GEE* unless they have earned it. There have been many a time when one of the boys will come to us and say, "Mom, Dad, I do not have enough money to cover the tax on the item I am getting, or for shipping, will you cover it for me?" Or they will ask "Mom, Dad, I only have $10 to cover the item, and it costs $14, can you cover the rest for me?" Most always, 99% of the time, we will cover that amount for them, as they are not only responsible enough to ask for help when they need it, but also as a way for them to learn generosity.

There are times, I must confess, when we have not had the time to get to the ATM machine or when money has been tight for us until we get our paychecks ourselves, that we have borrowed money from our children. This may seem like a foreign concept to some, but there is much for the boys to learn in the way of generosity, of loaning money, paying debts on time when we say we will, and that of interest when you borrow money. There are also still times, when our boys have no money, that if they want a small something and I have the cash on me, that I will give it to them as a means for them to have that physical experience of paying for something and making change.

Family Finances & Learning How to Handle GEE Through the Years

From the time our first son Chris was born, I have always believed in being very honest and open with our children about *GEE* and finances. My parents always kept income and finances some sort of sacred secret, feeling that I was not "old enough" to learn and know. While as an adult I respect that this was their way and I harbor no ill feelings regarding it, I do feel that by not allowing me to fully experience *GEE* both personally and as a family unit, that it left me in the dark once I was adult and on my own. The conditions then for me as an adult on my own were so that I had to learn as I went and very late in life, therefore causing me financial hardships that if I had been able to fully experience earlier on in life that I feel I would have been able to handle in another way with more knowledge and experience.

I have always known that what I wanted for our children was complete honesty when it comes to *GEE* and finances. But, my honesty goes with all topics, not just with *GEE*. I go into a more in-depth discussion about that level honesty in chapter twelve.

What I found myself doing with our children is being honest, and allowing them to help me with bills and even having them budget with me each month, rather than just saying "bills need to be paid, so we have no extra money." I have found that this is a wonderful Life Long Learning tool that can be used to assist our children to learn to be productive members of society. Rather than waiting until our children are deemed by society's influence or standards as "old enough", I say why not now? Who is to say that our children are not capable of learning and utilizing these concepts? Financial concepts, if they so desire, should be learned when the child feels they should learn them, as with all things in life.

We, as a family, discuss frequently and openly about how much the bills are ~ such as the mortgage, the cable bill, and the food bill etc. are each time they are to be paid. They also have asked to go online with me to see the checking account ~ it's balance and to pay bills with me online. They have also wanted to learn how to write a check to someone. All of these are things that when our children have asked, I have embraced and learned right along with them, enabling them to grasp and utilize these concepts now, so that they may know how to handle themselves as financially independent men as they grow.

Taking a simple trip to the store, in which your children have the opportunity to put together a grocery list and buy the groceries from start to finish, is also an excellent way to learn about budgeting, needs or wants, price comparing and much more. Our boys will often go shopping with us as well. We make a list of what items we need, then go together. They evaluate with us how much each item on the list is and we comparison shop, looking at if one brand is more or less than another and which is the better buy based upon weight or price and other factors. When the items are rung up at the register, they get to see first hand just exactly how much our food bill is and how much will then come off of the budget each time we go.

The complete remodel of our home was yet another way for us to embrace learning as Life Long Learners. While under construction, we lived in our home, therefore, our children learned how a home is built from the ground up. Everything from the actual financing of the remodel, to the demolition, to the "bare bones" of what tools it takes to build a home, to decorating, you name it. Our children learned price comparing, budgeting, spending, and saving while shopping for carpet, tile, and kitchen cabinetry.

The subsequent sale of our home a year and a half later, proved to show to our children the home buying and selling process with all of it's intimate details. Every minute detail from beginning to end Chris, Matthew, and Anthony were apart of ~ from what a mortgage is to the process of inspections, to how the loan qualifying process works etc., much more than I could ever write here. They learned all of this just simply by living it.

A mother once wrote the following about her experiences with her children when it comes to *GEE* and paying bills:

"Every pay day is "running" day for us. Being that the children are home with me, this means they go with me to do this. I find the fact that they must do the traveling means their day is being affected and disrupted. So instead them being bored and miserable, they become a part of the day and apart of the responsibilities. Of course, they love to be helpers, so I allow them to do just that. Being that my daughter is only three, she likes to help me make my daily lists. She 'writes' the lists, and then tells me what is on them. This may be for where we need to go, and is also for the groceries. I always try to keep mental note of what she tells me is on there so that I can be sure to accommodate some of what she puts. Such as carrots and dip (her favorite) or brownies, or what type of juice she wants. This allows her to feel important and an active appreciated part of the family choices. My son, being older helps me with the dollar amount part of things a lot. After going to the bank he will keep a notebook and open with him. He will write down the money amount we are beginning with ... after each stop and bill paid, he will subtract what we spent for me. This allows him to truly visualize and understand where the money goes, and why. We always discuss what is being paid, and why it is important and/or necessary for each thing paid. Such as, electric bill, or phone bill, or rent. The last stop we always make is the grocery store. He already knows ahead of time what amount of money is left for shopping, since he did the budgeting along the way. As we shop with our list both children will help choose the items and put them in the cart. Well, my point is, I keep my children, even the youngest, involved. I allow them to make their choices and give their input. But I also have them help me, so they gain an understanding of where the money goes. So there are never empty comments of "we do not have the money." My son especially now has a very mature understanding of what "bills need paying" means. He sees, on paper, how the money dwindles down each week. We discuss freely the importance of what each bill paid is for. He may not understand yet the complications ... but he knows we cannot drive our car unless we pay to keep that license plate on it and the car insurance paid. "What insurance?" he asks. I say, "Insurance is so that if there is a car accident, the insurance company helps pay

for the expensive damages and/or doctor bills." The phone bill needs to be paid so that we can have the phone to keep in touch with friends and family. Cable bill ... well, you have your favorite shows, and we have ours. If I do not pay for the cable, we will not be able to watch them".

There will come a time in the not so distant future that we will not need to be relying upon the skills of *GEE* to make it mean what it does to us now. We are coming into a time where we will view *GEE* as more of an energy exchange, rather than the piece of paper that we hold so dear to our hearts at this time. In this new era we are entering into now, I envision a time in which we return back to the roots of our ancestors and will begin to barter and trade for items without a certain value being placed upon their worth. In this new era, I envision that we will begin to give to one another of our gifts, talents, and "stuff" that we have freely without a monetary connotation to it. In trading and bartering, we will not place weight on whether a chicken is worth more than a horse, it will be just an exchange of what it is that we each have to give, of what the other needs, and we will be accepting of this. Until such time, these are tools to be here for you to utilize within Life Long Learning to show us the many paths that can be offered within *GEE* as it is now in society.

~

We cannot form our children on our concepts; we must take them and love them as they are given to us
~ Johann Wolfgang von Goethe

Chapter Seven

The Little Black Box ~
Life Long Learning and the World of Television

To T.V. or Not to T.V.? That is the Question...

Ah! The world of television! There has been much discussion and heated debate as to T.V. or not to T.V. Some experts say it will rot your child's brain and that there is too much violence on television and that it is the evil of this world. Others advocate the first amendment right here in the United States of free speech and that it is up to the parents to regulate what their children watch and do not watch on television.

I believe I am somewhere in-between really. I believe there is no one right answer to this debate. While agree that maybe there is far too much what society terms as negativity on television these days, I also feel that there is a basic right as human beings on this planet to speak our truth as we perceive it and that the laws here in the United States and other countries provide for that freedom. However what I do not agree with is that it is the parents' responsibility to be the gatekeeper of the remote control or to "regulate" what children watch.

Now, I know that this may be breaking the mold and that some people may be up in arms screaming at me right about now, but I feel that each individual is responsible for finding their own balance with regard to the little (or in some homes big) black box with a screen called a television set. Yes, this also means children too. Children are the same as us adults in that they have and can express their own preferences, likes and dislikes, and therefore should not be restricted to the viewing content on the television simply because we say so because "we are the adult". Who are we to say what type of programming is better than the other for our children? The only and best judge of which type of programming they will enjoy, learn from, and wish to watch is the child themselves. *BUT.....BUT....* you say, what about violence? What about "educating" our children via the T.V.? Is it not my responsibility as a parent to shelter them from the garbage on television today? What if they are not "old enough" to understand something on T.V.? My answer to those questions is how else will they learn what is garbage and considered non-educational *if* they do not have the chance to experience the contrasts for themselves? Do we really wish for our children to grow up believe that something is supposedly good or bad for them simply because an adult or other authority figure says so? Do we not want our children to be able to research things out for themselves and then make an informed choice based upon all of the information rather than only parts of it?

As far as whether or not we feel or do not feel that a child is "old enough" or "ready" for the concepts that are brought forth upon a particular program, my thoughts are simply this...... children are quite inept people, because that is who they are, individuals just like you and I. If a concept is something that is beyond their capability or reasoning to grasp, then the child will ask questions. It will be then up to you as their guide, to give that child the answers they seek, to the best of your capability. And if you do not know the answers, it is up to you to direct them to where they can find those answers.

Children do not ask questions and/or view anything in life, television or anything else in life that they are not ready for. They are their best gauges for their own growth. If the content being shown is not to their liking or they feel uncomfortable enough with what is on, they will simply turn it off, or they will change the station to find something else that interests them. It is the very same thing we do, our children are the same. They should be allotted the same freedoms and respect over their own growth, including television viewing as we have. We would not like it if someone came into the living room and shut the T.V. off telling us that we cannot watch what is on because we are not "old enough" or not "ready" to watch it? If someone were to do that to you, you would feel insulted, disrespected, and feel as if that person had no right to tell you what is appropriate for you to watch or not to watch, that this should be your choice. Yet, this is exactly how our children feel when we do this very same thing to them.

I can remember how the concept of asking questions on programs that we may feel our children are not ready for came to light one night for us as a family to show this life lesson to us. One evening, while watching a movie together as a family, I soon had a feeling that maybe Matthew and Anthony, five and a half and 7 at the time, might not grasp what was going on in the movie and that one or both of them would fall asleep possibly from boredom from "not getting it". Surely, Chris being older would surely "get" the movie and may not at all need anything explained to him, but our younger two, I was not so sure. Much to my surprise, all of them became engrossed in the film, absorbing the information in it and following the story line as if they were sponges soaking up anything and everything about the movie. During the movie, both Matthew and Anthony began asking all sorts of questions. That is when the light bulb turned on for me! WOW!! I thought. Here is a wonderful Life Long Learning moment in which something that I thought was going to be a total bust, turned out to be a beautiful learning time for us as a family.

It is so ironically funny how sometimes it takes "Ah Ha" moments like this to transform our lives. Many years ago, before we became a Life Long Learning family, my husband and I would restrict and "regulate" everything that our boys watched, especially our two younger ones. We had held the belief back then (and this was also the teacher in me) that we thought for sure that we would need to until they were "old enough" not watch certain shows or certain TV stations. Looking back now on this, I see just how ridiculous it all was, how much time and energy I was wasting in trying supposedly to protect them from what I thought at the time was the "big, bad T.V."

Since that time, I have learned that children will, just as ours have, find balance in television viewing on their own, *if* you give them the freedom and space to do so. I actually had seen evidence of this with Chris, although at the time, I did not know that this was what actually happening and that that was what I was actually doing. When he was younger, true I did regulate, as in control, what he watched but I never really "regulated" how much, I always let him do that on his own. And there would be many a time when he would sit and watch Barney for what seemed like *hours*. In retrospect though, even though he may have watched for all those hours, he learned *so* much from that one little half hour show of Barney, much more than I ever realized. In addition to what we were modeling as a family at home and the learning he was receiving at home in those toddler years, Barney was actually reinforcing all of that he learned, in addition to introducing and reinforcing other Life Long Learning concepts that he would never have learned all from just myself or my husband showing him.

There were also time that I would find that "Barney" or whatever show was on at the time was just on as what I would call "background" watching. In other words, the show would be on while in the background, while he happily played with his blocks or built science experiments or whatever he was into learning at that moment. To be honest, I truly believe that this is how Chris has developed the ability to multitask. Most boys, and subsequently, most men, are not able to multitask because they are left brain coordinated, which is that they are only able to focus on one task at a time. Boys and men in society are "stereotyped" as they say. That stereotype also says that most girls and women are more right brained than boys and men are. However, being that Chris had this type of environment within his early years of learning, and also our other two, Matthew and Anthony, it is remarkable to see that truly Chris is quite capable and efficient in multitasking.

With Chris, as he grew though, we never had to sit him down and explained to him that we were "letting him balance his television viewing", it just happened on its' own. He learned to find that balance all on his own. We would always discuss with him what shows we would like to see him watch, but we let go of telling him what he could and could not watch. He would always choose, just as he still does to this day what shows he felt were/are appropriate for him to explore and which he feels uncomfortable with and watches accordingly.

"Deschooling" and Balancing the T.V.

I must say that with Matthew and Anthony, things were much different when they were younger. As the teacher in me became more prevalent in their younger years, we did impose a "regulating" of sorts when they were in "school", of what they could watch. So, when the time came as a Life Long Learning family, to begin our "deschooling" of the T.V. viewing and begin opening the doors of possibilities with them finding their own balance in television land, we felt it was somewhat necessary to have a family discussion about the matter. We sat down with Matthew and Anthony and explained to them that they could watch what they wish to on T.V., that we believed that they were responsible enough to know what shows are worthwhile viewing for them and which were not and for how long to watch the television, that they are free to make that choice, to find that balance on their own. We also did suggest that there were certain programs we did not feel were the best choice in our view, why we felt they were not and that our preference is that they do not watch them, but that ultimately the choice was theirs.

Now of course, their first reaction was the obvious one. Being that they felt free, as if they had somehow been caged animals and were about to be released into the wild again for the first time since their capture into the world of restriction of television land, they did what any children would have done under these circumstances ~ they began to watch that little black box whatever whenever as a means to "test" us to see if we were *really* serious about giving them the freedom to choose their own T.V. viewing! It became and stayed that way for many months a television fest! They would watch shows like Inuyahsa, Dragonball Z, and He-man, virtually anything on Cartoon Network because with the exception of Scooby Doo or Pokemon or Yu-Gi-Oh, we really did not "allow" them to watch Cartoon Network before our "deschooling" of the little black box. They also began watching T.V. for hours and hours on end, as if they were afraid somehow that if they were to stop watching, that we would end up pulling the plug and go back to the old ways of "restriction" again.

At one point, my husband started to question the validity of our approach, as he thought it "crazy" as to how much T.V. they were watching and what they were watching. Of course, my response to him was always, "Please, just be patient with them and with our approach to this, it will all come full circle, you will see, just trust and have faith that all will be as it should be in time." I commend my husband for his love, trust, faith, and the incredible amount of patience he had with our boys and with me. He has been, we have been, rewarded beyond measure in what transpired.

At some point, hard to remember exactly when, an amazing thing occurred, in which we knew that all of our trust, faith, and patience had indeed come full circle and gave us our life's reward. It seems that as time went on and even in the now as I write this book, we have found that our boys are watching other stations, other than just Cartoon Network. We find too that they do not watch nearly as much television as they once did. In fact all of what they do watch has value and learning in it, as we too, as parents, in "deschooling" the T.V. found that there is learning in everything on this little black box we call a television set.

When we were at my mother-in-law's house one time, my brother-in-law, had what I would consider to be a rather sexually explicit show on, all three of our boys chose to leave the room without any of us there (including my mother-in-law, my father-in-law or my brother-in-law) having to say a word. Our boys, in their learning of how to balance for themselves that little black box, found themselves in a situation where there was a movie that others in the room were watching that they did not feel comfortable watching, and one by one, starting first with our oldest son, walked out of the room, stating that they were going to play video games. In fact, I recall it being so cute, so innocent and sweet, as Chris turned to Anthony and said "Hey bro, let's go see if Uncle Robbie will let us play some video games on his T.V. in his room." We both, my husband and I, felt so much pride in our boys that day and deep down this gave us both the confirmation that we were on the right path with our children.

I have to say overall, that our boys watch of their own volition, some quite intriguing shows and learn many, many things from television viewing. All of which are useful life learning tools that they can utilize in the here and now and as they grow, for a lifetime. Disney Channel is *still* our boys' favorite station (even Chris whom is almost 14 now!) and there are some real family and life value shows on there that we as a family learn so much from. My husband and I too, have also learned from our boys that the shows that we once thought were so horrible, have just as much to learn on them as the supposedly "good" ones. It is all in how one perceives the world that the world then is.

Take for example the Cartoon Network show *Totally Spies*. In that show, we learned a science experiment of how to make soap float. And here I always thought it was some just "spy show" and my husband thought it was a "girly" show. This brings to light another wonderful aspect of our Life Long Learning together as a family. In watching television programming together and when they watch on their own, our boys do not make any sexist type or age specific type distinctions stating that "oh this show I would never watch because it is a "girl's" show", or that show is for "babies", nor do they only watch "boy" shows. They watch *all* shows, and embrace them for the learning value of them, regardless of whether it is marketed for a specific audience or not. Chris will be all to happy to tell anyone that he still enjoys watching *Rugrats, Lambchop, or Yu-Gi-Oh* just as well as he likes to watch *Seven Heaven or Charmed*. From a parental standpoint I am glad, because he should be able to enjoy all television programming, free of the ridicule he used to receive back within the schooling environment for being considered "geeky" or "weird" simply because he chooses to like what he chooses to like. I mean, heck, my husband and I love to watch *Sponge Bob, Yu-Gi-oh, and Rugrats*!

There are still times that my husband and I even come across a show that we think they might find interesting, we would say, "Hey boys, turn to channel (whatever) to see how cool this (whatever it is we were/are watching) is", "or come into our room, you got to see this!" and we would watch the program together. Or there are times when we will tape something a program of interest and then later watch it as a family show or movie night. We will then as we watch it together, explore, hypothesize and ask questions and discover the possible answers as a family.

I just recently did this with a show I taped for Anthony. As I spoke of previously, Anthony has an avid interest in dogs. Since he could walk and talk, he has always said he wants to be as he put it when he was a toddler, "A doggie doctor". He has since revised that to say that he wants to utilize herbal medicine and alternative healing methods to help all animals as a Veterinarian. He loves animals of all kinds, but as a particular affinity and connection to dogs. Thus, when a show on *KPBS* here came on all about the origin and history of dogs, naturally I taped it and we watched it together later that afternoon. It became a fascinating learning for both of us on not only how the dog came into existence, but about the study of DNA strands and how scientists are helping breeders to pinpoint the potentially harmful DNA in order to hopefully not pass on genes that will make inbred dogs sick with certain diseases. We also learned about how this scientific work with dogs DNA is now helping researchers in the fight many of the same human diseases such as cancer and narcolepsy that we share in common with dogs.

In reality though, our boys do not watch nearly the amount of television that they did when we first started "deschooling" the television. They do not spend hardly any time at all watching television, and when they do anymore, it is usually what society terms as "educational" in nature. The boys find on whole that they enjoy other activities such as riding their scooters at the park across the street from our house, going on a nature exploration hike in the pond area by our house, sketching, playing a board game, or just hanging out as brothers or as a family together and talking with one another as more valuable than the television.

Saying that children should be able to have self-discovery upon their television viewing is not to say that there should be or will be this pandemonium and free-for-all going on within your home. And it is also not to say that we cannot provide choices. By all means, what is our responsibility as parents, and as a Life Long Learning family is to provide as many choices to our children as is available and possible for us to bring forth to them. There have been many examples shown here within this chapter, to show that this indeed can be done. It is by all means ok for you to suggest a certain program or certain type of programming or station. You can even explain to your child your own preferences as to which programs you may wish them to view and what your reasons are for your preferences. However, the ultimate choice as to a child's television viewing should reside with our children.

Remember, give your child choice in life and it opens the whole world up to them, where literally **anything** is and can be possible! It gives our children the ability to utilize the power within them to manifest anything in life. Placing of restrictions, whether it be on the television, or on anything in life, and the never ending chants of the "You cant's" or "You can only do this and that", only makes that restriction becomes more enticing to them, making them **want** to do it even more simply because it is in our nature as human beings to question why? or why not? By allowing for the choice to come from with them, this then takes the power away from the alluring "thing" whatever it is that they want to do, and places it back where it truly belongs, inside of them. Ultimately a child will then not wish to choose to do whatever was once forbidden, as that forbidden item, whatever it was, has no power anymore, they do. The ultimate power in all of us, lies within us.

~

Be who you are, say what you feel, those who mind do not matter and those who matter do not mind

~ Dr. Seuss

Chapter Eight

Taking a Ride Along the Information Super Highway!

In today's rapidly growing world, the internet can be an invaluable resource as a Life Long Learning family. Take for example, my middle son, Matthew, asked in a conversation while we were painting our home one day (as we were getting it ready to be sold), "Mom, who invented paint?" And of course, with the snap of my fingers, I knew the answer right away? Because I am a mom and I am suppose to know everything right?!

Ha! No, in fact, I rather did *not* know the answer. I cannot lay claim to the fact that I know everything. No one person can. Although, what I did say to him was that we could research it. Which is where the internet came in. Rather than making a trip to the library, which one can certainly do and has enormous benefits on it's own, we chose to go upstairs to do the next best thing, the World Wide Web. From that short jaunt, we learned how to research on the internet together and learned all about "Who invented paint", which then turned into more research on the Egyptians, as they were one of the first people to utilize the concept of paint with the different pigments in the soil, to draw hieroglyphics.

This then, turned into a conversation with my youngest son Anthony, about other individuals whom invented other things, yet the next day. While driving, he noticed the street sweeper and he asked "Mommy, who invented the street sweeper?" As such, when we got home, what did we do? Sure enough! We researched it on the internet, only to find that Charles Brooks invented not only the street sweeper, but two very important items that we still use today ~ the trash receptacle and the paper hole punch.

We have had Pokemon cards that have been written in a language that none of us knew which language or what the card said, only to find that when we were able to research a translator program online, we were not only able to find out that it was actually written in Italian (we thought it might be Spanish actually!), but we were also able to find out what the words were translated into.

We have also played learning games online, gone on virtual field trips, (I will provide the information about where to access this in the resources section at the end of this book) and found out some amazing facts online. From facts about Mars and all about *NASA*, to how to sketch pokemon, to learning how to spell words.

We also do **alot** of reading online. I can remember when we first started being a Life Long Learning family that Chris, whom was always told while in the schooling environment that he was a terrible reader and could not comprehend anything, read a thirty-two chapter book on the internet within two days! Some of our closest cuddling moments are when we are snuggling in bed together reading a fascinating article online. Like a few months back when we discovered an article about the game Mancala. Mancala is an ancient Egyptian game that dates back thousands of years and has traveled the globe under different names in different countries. It is now a game that our boys love to play. Had it not been for finding that article online, we would have possibly never known what the game Mancala was!

Another way that they internet can be utilized as a Life Long Learning tool is that of the internet auction site of *Ebay*. Our children have also recently discovered *Ebay*. Being on *Ebay* and bid for small priced things (nothing that Chris, Matthew, or Anthony has ever bid on has been more than 15 *GEE's* or $15.00) the money that has been given to them for birthdays and holidays has been a wonderful real life learning experience. When Matthew first found *Ebay*, and did not know what it was or how it worked. Daddy proceeded to explain to him that it was like how he learned to bid for properties when playing the board game *Monopoly* or playing the Nintendo Gamecube version of *Monopoly* called *Monopoly Party*. In both games, when a player does not choose to purchase a given property, it goes up for auction. It is then bid on and the highest bidder wins.

Aaron went onto further explain that this is how it works in real life on the internet – that people just like himself, whom have items to sell place them up for auction, and people just like him bid for them using the money that they have. As our children have come to learn, that they bid whatever money they wish to out of the money they have and that they cannot bid more than the money that they have. Our boys have also come to learn perseverance in that if they are out bid on a particular item, that they can always search again for a similar item to bid upon and that maybe they will win the bid on that item.

The art of patience has also been learned by our children, as they know that they sometimes need to wait as much as a week or more in some cases, to find out if they have won a bid. They have also learn patience in that if they have lost a bid on something, that it is ok and not then end of the world. Patience also in the fact that they may need to wait for a time until a similar item like the one they may have lost the auction on may come on *Ebay*, however, it may be days, weeks, or months before it does. It has shown our children too, that waiting for something is ok, and that everything is not always handed to you right then and there. Sometimes you do have to wait or find another item that is comparable.

I can honestly say that I am quite grateful for my brother, Vince. Being in the computer field, Vince has had his share of extra computers and computer parts; therefore, we are lucky enough to have each of our boys a computer in their own rooms. I can hear what you are saying already, "Oh my! They each have computers with internet access that they can be online 24/7?" Yes, they do each have their own computers and yes, they can access the internet 24/7. Again, this goes back to what I have written previously, that children need to be able to have the freedom to make their own choices in life, just as we adults do. Remember, giving your child choice in life and it opens the whole world up to them, where literally anything is possible! It gives our children the ability to utilize the power within them to manifest anything in life.

So, yes, our children do have their own computers with internet access available to them at anytime they want to, wish to, or need to utilize it. How else with they learn how to navigate the world wide web and that of how to find what it is they wish to learn in life, if they do not learn first hand on their own and if they do not have as many resources available to them as possible?

"But…what about internet security? And what about websites that you do not want them visiting and information that you do not want them giving out online?" All three of our children know that if they come to a website that does not feel right to them or has content that is not what they are looking for but that makes them feel uncomfortable, that they can either choose to come let us know. Or they cannot choose the delete, backspace, or x buttons to remove that content off of their computer. Rather than punishing them for stumbling across a site that is what may be considered inappropriate, we would simply inquire as to if they know how they got to that site if they knew, and then ensure that it becomes a blocked website on their computer through the router, so they will not be able to access it again if that is what they choose since it makes them feel uncomfortable. It would also give us pause to have a discussion as to why they may feel that the website is inappropriate.

As far as giving out information online via IM (Instant Messenger) or when purchasing something or signing up for something online, we have discussed with and all of our children know that if someone whom they do not know shows up on their IM, they do not respond, they simply go to the feature (which we have shown them how to do) that blocks that user from being able to IM them again. They all know that this is for their safety and is something that has never been an issue. They also know that if there ever is a problem that they can come to us, and they indeed do.

When it comes to purchases, we have never had to tell our boys directly that they need to come to us first, they have always used their common sense and good judgment to know and always do come to us to ask us permission before signing up online for something. Chris at almost 14 years old, still does this to this day, and he has been online now actively for almost 6 years plus now, he still comes to me when he wants to sign up online for something.

With anything internet related, we have had complete faith and trust within our children. They have found some amazing sites that we would have never found had it not been for their researching.

Chris has become a computer genius, due to having had his own computer since the age of four. He has learned website design, how to take apart and put back together almost any computer. He has learned to install software, troubleshoot, and repair pretty much any PC you give to him. In truth, he knows more than his dad about computers and my husband is also in the computer industry! Anytime there is something wrong with my computer, I simply call Chris and walla! It is like magic! he fixes it. As I have written back in chapter four, it is one of his life passions.

All of our children have their own email addresses, something very rare these days. While most parents have their own email addresses, they simply think that their children can "wait until they are old enough to learn how, they do not need an email address now. My question is, why not? In this age of computers and it being the wave of the future, I believe that it is imperative that our children, if they express an interest in learning, should learn as much as they can about how a computer works from the inside and out. Learning to utilize the internet is only one piece to this complex puzzle. As is learning to email a letter online.

Our children, as a direct result of having their own email addresses have learned how to write a letter by emailing, have learned how to download programs online, and how to send files via email in attachments and more! All of this has been on their own, with only guidance and assistance by my husband and I when asked. They have wanted to learn and I know that in the now and as they continue to grow, this knowledge is and will continue to be a valuable resource for them in their lives. They will be all the better for learning now how to research and find what it is they need via one of the most economical and fastest means available at our fingertips today.

Some parents feel that children should not have internet available to them 24/7, that they should restrict their viewing the internet, as they would restrict viewing the television. Again, I ask why? Why would we ever restrict learning in any form? Whether it be just what we would consider "messing around" by playing a video game online or just emailing a friend that is learning. No matter what package on the world wide web it comes in, it is still knowledge, it is still learning. That knowledge and that learning then turns into wisdom. And if we are, and our children are able then to take that learning at utilize it in any form in life, then why would we wish to restrict that.

Besides which, how would we feel if all of the sudden after let's say one hour of being online, and we were right in the middle of a really informative webpage, would we like it if someone came in and said, "Ok, you must get off the computer now, your time is up, no more learning for you tonight!". We would not like it one bit. We do not police ourselves or other adults in this manner, stating when we can or cannot be online and for how long. When we go online, we stay on as long as we wish. That may be until dinner gets made or until we are sleepy and are ready for bed, but nonetheless, it is until we **choose** to stop being online, not because someone has forced us to get offline. Therefore, don't our children deserve the same ability to choose for themselves? Do they not deserve the same respect to make those choices as we give to ourselves?

The information super highway…Just like that of the road of life, the internet is an invaluable resource to us all on our Life Long Learning path.

~

Once you start to question your life, you get to a higher level of awareness. It's like turning a light on ~ voila! You see you have choices and choices are sacred ~ Naomi Judd

Chapter Nine

Let's Play Some Games!

Do you remember as a child playing the game of *Life*? Or how about *Parcheesi* or *Scrabble*? Do you remember all of the fun, new, and exciting things that you learned from these games? Things such as ~ the unlimitless options in the game of *Life*, or the skills of strategy and critical thinking in that of *Parcheesi*; or how about the spelling, reading, and language skills of *Scrabble*.

Games can provide such a vast array of Life Long Learning possibilities! The possibilities are truly endless. And what better way to learn then to make it into a fun game! Board games such as *Egyptians* provide learning on levels from that of trading and bartering all the way to information about the Egyptian leaders of those times. This can lead to a further pursuit of Egyptian culture, archeology, hieroglyphics, the ancient study of the pyramids and much more!

Oh Happy Day! Let's Learn Through Play!

As small children, the way we all learn is through play. There is even a commercial made by the California Children and Families Commission that states about how important it is for us as parents to play with our children when they babies until the age of five as playing stimulates their creativity and gets them "ready" for school because a child's brain develops the most during these five years. I actually find this commercial to be somewhat amusing, simply because our brains, our cognitive ability continues to grow from the day we are born until the day we draw our last breath here on this earth. Yes, we may develop rapidly on a physical during these first five years, but why is it that the first five years are the only years important here? Why are not **all** of our learning years, for as long as we live, our whole life long, just as important?

It is as if the government is saying that play with your children for the first five years of their lives, and the rest of their childhood, teen years and onward, really does not matter, it does not continue a foundation of learning after age six and they will then learn from "school" and nowhere else! Do they **really** believe that we stop learning once we reach "compulsory educational age" and that they only way we will learn is if someone "teaches in school" us from age six on? Sadly, the answer is yes, they do actually believe this. What is even sadder still is the fact that the government projects this image onto us and expects that because they say it is so, that it is, and we as a societal whole buy into these notions, never questioning, never thinking freely for ourselves anything outside of the box that the government places us in.

We, as a society, are more and more, losing our rights to be free. Here in the United States, we are "taught" that we are a free country, and yet, we really are only free within the confines of what the government says is free. This then, is not true freedom. We may be **freer** than most other country's on this planet, however, we are not the "free" society that our government claims and projects us to be in its' truest of forms.

It is really through play, and all forms of play and exploration, that we can learn the best. Of course, this is not to say that it is the only way in which we learn, but it is truly one of the best.

The "Opoly's"!

There are just so many games available nowadays to learn with and from. From the classics like *Monopoly* to video and computer games. Yes, I did say video and computer games. I will speak more about those later, but first.....The good old fashioned board games.

Classics like *Monopoly* have really transformed over the years. The days of just your standard *Monopoly* versions are **long** gone. Oh yes, there is still the classic *Monopoly*, of course, but now there are also many other versions to expand upon the "opoly" learning. There is an "opoly" for just about everything now! You have your *Spaceopoly*, your *Cat-in-the-Hatopoly*, your *Constructionopoly*, and your *Stock Market Tycoonopoly*. Geez, they even have a *Make Your Own Monopoly*, where all of the pieces and a blank board game are there but you design your own "opoly" game! And of course, there is our favorite here in our house of the *Disneylandoploy* and the *Dogopoly*! You name it; there is probably an "opoly" for it! The really wonderful and amazing thing is that there is so much you can learn from these variations of this classic game. You can learn how to make it in the

Stock Market, or build your own .com monopoly, or even learn about the herbivores and the carnivores of the dinosaur world.

We have here at our home, a small but growing collection of both the board game version and the video and computer game versions of the "opoly's". One of the awesome things that occurred on our "opoly" adventures was that our children actually got to take the board game version of *Monopoly* and apply it in a "real life" hands-on application of their learning. As, I explained this more in-depth in the previous chapter, *Ebay* was a way to take the learning from the "opoly's" and apply it in a real life experience, because what is the absolute best way to learn, is that of through experience, through living it and actually doing it.

From the *Stock Market Tycoonopoly*, if one has the means to do so, you can go online and set up a brokerage account with your children (under your name of course!) and buy, sell, and trade stocks in real time, taking from what you and your children learned within the game itself and applying it in real life and being able to assimilate and discuss the similarities and the distinctions between the game and the real life examples.

Games, Games, and More Games!

There are yet many other learning board games as well to expand your knowledge on just about anything you wish to learn. One of our favorite board games, is a game called *Kanji*. In *Kanji*, you can learn to count in Japanese from one to ten, learning to say, write, and read the ancient symbols for Japanese numbers. This along with many other Japanese items of interest has helped our boys to learn the culture, customs, and traditions of the Japanese. Another one of our favorite games to play is that of *Mad Math*. *Mad Math* uses strategy and calculation to learn all four of the major forms of math. Classic games such as *Scrabble* and a variation of that game on the computer called *Text Twist* are also household favorites here. Both utilize letters to enable each player to spell words and twist letters around to form words.

All three of out boys love this game *Text Twist*. It was twenty *GEE's* ($20) and it was the best money that we have ever spent, as the saying goes. I remember one time when Anthony and I played this game and the letters that came up were *A R N U E and L*. He found the word 'learn' all by himself and screamed out "Mommy! I found the word 'learn'! Look *L E A R N*!" I sure did not see that word in there, but he did! It is wonderful to be able to pull out of the various words out of just a simple group of letters. Along those same lines, Wheel of Fortune is another wonderful game. Board game version and/or video/computer game versions provide many hours of word twisting fun!

Games need not be that elaborate or prepackaged either to have learning involved. *Dominos* are a simple but yet wonderful way to learn so many things from math, to geometry, to number to amount correspondence. Also learning of stacking and strategic thinking when building a valley of dominos and then checking to see if they all fall as they are intended to, is also a Life Long Learning experience that is one not to miss! There are so many intricate designs and patterns that can be created with dominos. There is also much history that can be learned about how the domino came into existence.

The actual word *"Domino"* is a French word for a black and white hood worn by Catholic priests in winter. The oldest domino sets date back to around 1120 A.D. *Dominoes*, as most of the Western world knows them; however, appear to be a Chinese invention. The name of the inventor cannot be traced. The domino game appeared first in Europe in 18th Century Italy, possibly in the courts of Venice and Naples. Although domino tiles are clearly of Chinese inheritance, there is debate over whether the game played by Europeans was brought by the Chinese to Europe in the fourteenth century or, in fact, was invented independently.

Another simple and yet many faceted learning to is that of playing cards. A basic game of *Blackjack*, or 21, provides basic math skills that I have had the pleasure of play with not only my own children from a young age, but also showing a child as little as the age of three basic math skills from. Now, I know what you may be thinking…..what is this woman trying to do, make early gamblers out of our children, by promoting a card game played in major casinos around the globe! Quite the contrary. Actually, while *Blackjack* may be played in casinos around the globe, it is also a key game in learning strategy, critical thinking, and basic math skills. It was this long before it became a game to win money at your local casino. Card games in various forms have been around since the 10th century. The earliest playing cards are believed to have originated in Central Asia. The documented history of card playing began in the 10th century, when the Chinese began using paper dominoes by shuffling and dealing them in new games. Four suited decks with court cards evolved in the Moslem world and were imported by Europeans before 1370. In those days, cards were hand painted and only the very wealthy could afford them, but with the invention of woodcuts in the 14th century, Europeans began mass production.

It is from French designs that the cards we use today are derived. France gave us the suits of spades, clubs, diamonds and hearts, and the use of simple shapes and flat colors helped facilitate manufacture. French cards soon flooded the market and were exported in all directions. They became the standard in England first, and then in the British Colonies of America.

Americans began making their own cards around 1800. Yankee ingenuity soon invented or adopted practical refinements: double headed court cards (to avoid the nuisance of turning the figure upright), varnished surfaces (for durability and smoothness in shuffling), indexes (the identifying marks placed in the cards' borders or corners), and rounded corners (which avoid the wear that card players inflict on square corners).

Here in our home, we must have, no joke, at least twenty to twenty-five decks of cards! Many varieties from Dolphins and lighthouse cards, to Legoland, to the basic Bicycle cards. *UNO*, is another card game that we love to play as a Life Long Learning family. We have the classic *UNO*, Sesame Street *UNO* and even Harry Potter *UNO*. A man by the name of Merle Robbins is the actual inventor of the *UNO* game. He was an Ohio barbershop owner, and like us here in our family, loved to play cards. One day in 1971, Merle came up with the idea for *UNO* and introduced the game to his family. When his family and friends began playing *UNO* more and more, Merle took notice. He and his family decided to pool together $8,000 and have 5,000 games made. Believe it or not, that's how *UNO* got its start!

So how did *UNO* go from 5,000 games to 125 million? At first, Merle sold *UNO* from his barbershop. A few friends and local businesses sold them, too. Then *UNO* took the next step towards card game fame: Merle sold the *UNO* rights to a funeral parlor owner and *UNO* fan from Joliet, Illinois. The cost? Fifty thousand dollars, plus royalties of 10 cents per game. International Games Inc. was then formed to market *UNO*, and sales skyrocketed. In 1992, International Games became part of the Mattel family, and *UNO* had a new home. And that is how *UNO* became the huge success that it is today! Amazing, all from a man who had a vision and brought his vision into his barbershop!

Baseball cards are yet another modality for learning. Matthew found a game online for $5, which we purchased and had shipped, to us. In this board game you can take each baseball players percentages,

RBI's (runs batted in), hitting and pitching averages; taking all of those and somehow create mathematical equations based upon the games complex formulas to divide, subtract, multiply, add, calculate other percentages and averages to play a nine inning game of baseball with strikes, balls, hits, doubles, homeruns and so for, utilizing only baseball cards and the information on them.

I have to say though, without a doubt, our two utmost favorite card games which involve so much learning, are that of a game called *Squish* and of course *Yu-Gi-Oh*. *Squish* is also known by many other names, I have since learned, and involves not only the skills of solitaire with multiple players, but also that of multiplication and addition and subtraction of negative and positive numbers.

The Little Card Game Called ~ Yu-Gi-Oh!

Yu-Gi-Oh is the other favorite within our family. Although, I think that it is more of a favorite as of late in our home than that of *Squish* at times! *Yu-Gi-Oh* is much more than just a card game though. As a Life Long Learning family, we have learned so much from this intrinsic card game. Like all card games, it is not limited to age, gender, or ability confines ~ as young, old, male, female, skilled and/or beginner can learn and play this game.

The creator of *Yu-Gi-Oh*, Kazuki Takahashi became passionate about drawing comics in his teens, and made his debut in Japan's best-selling weekly comic magazine, Shonen Jump, in 1991. After taking some time to recharge his artistic energy, he began drawing the comic series *Yu-Gi-Oh* in 1996. The animated version of *Yu-Gi-Oh* debuted in 2000 and became an immediate hit.

It certainly is a hit with our family! Takahashi gave inspiration to Matthew to create, illustrate, and write in his own words, his own card game. It is made out of simple pieces of paper, and is all hand made with some amazing sketch work, and he is quite proud of his card game he has invented. Our boys have explored many aspects of ancient Egypt ~ the culture and the customs of this country as well.

Some parents feel that *Yu-Gi-Oh* is too violent for their children to watch or to play as a game. For our children and for my husband, Aaron as well, they enjoy *Yu-Gi-Oh* not for the violence. In essence they do not view *Yu-Gi-Oh* as violent, because they are able to distinguish the difference between fantasy play and reality and know that *Yu-Gi-Oh* is fantasy. As far as the "battle" of it goes, they do not view it as battling as in hurting someone or something. They do not place the "labels" of good or bad, right or wrong to it, it is just what is for them. And what is is that they view *Yu-Gi-Oh* as learning, as fantasy and role-playing and just as plain old fun!

There is so much learning in *Yu-Gi-Oh*. There are addition and subtraction of multiple numbers from single digit all the way to four or more digits. Also, there is the added benefit of critical thinking skills, life strategy skills (i.e. ok, this way did not work, how else can I make this work), life perseverance skills (not giving up when your life points are down is a great way to learn perseverance), statistical skills (each of my boys know the statistical data of each of the *Yu-Gi-Oh* guys ~ much like that of baseball statistics), responsibility skills too ~ each one of them are responsible for maintaining their own cards ~ taking care of them and the natural consequences of taking care of or not taking care of something.

On watching the *Yu-Gi-Oh* show, they also learn friendship skills in addition to all of what I mentioned earlier ~ when a friend is in a bind on the show and needing help with something, they show within the program how friends stick by each other and brainstorm solutions on how to help their friends through what they are dealing with at that moment, until it is resolved. They also view the "attacks" and "battles" of what their monsters can do in a positive way, showing that through play, that they have a positive voice of power and change (in other words they have the power to change and transform their monsters, which gives them a sense of self confidence, perseverance, and self esteem to have the ability to change positively what is in their own lives and their own world) in the world that is from a child's perspective is dominated by adults in which they as children do not always feel they have a voice.

So, there is much more to this game than just the fact that there are monsters or violence. What is learned within this game are life building skills that children can utilize throughout their lies, not just for the length of time they spend playing the game. These are the things that my children see when they see, watch, and play *Yu-Gi-Oh*. They do not see it as violence ~ they look beyond the violence to see its true learning value.

As adults, sometimes we have a hard time seeing the true value of something, simply taking things as what we perceive is their initial face value i.e. only seeing *Yu-Gi-Oh* as violent, out of fear of the unknown....out of fear of delving deeper into the possibility of what something could really mean for it's positive, rather than negative value, and seeing it for the value that our children hold within it, through their eyes. It is only when we free ourselves to delve deeper into, around, through and viewing all sides of something that we are free to see what it's true possibility can be and is, making the fear of the unknown and what our initial perceptions of something are transformed.

So, this card game called *Yu-Gi-Oh*, has given us so much more than just purchasing and playing with a bunch of cards. It has enabled our boys to forge a bond with their father unlike any other that they have had before. The quality time they have spent together collecting, talking for hours about, playing and learning together, and being in awe of these cards is priceless and immeasurable. Takahashi put it so well, when he spoke in an interview with *Time.com*, when he said, *".....the main thing I want them to understand is if you combine the "yu" in Yugi and the "jo" in Jounouchi [the main character's best friend], you get the word yujo. Yujo translates into the word "Friendship" in English, but it is actually more powerful than that. If children get a strong sense of friendship among the characters in the story, and bring that forth into their own lives, then I will be happy."*

On the Road Again

Speaking of games, there are many, many games you can play while on the road. Whether you are traveling just to the grocery store or going on a cross-country trip, there are plenty of games you can play that increase the learning while on the road. I highly recommend Diane Flynn Keith's book, *Carschooling.* As Diane says on her website about her book *Carschooling* *".... (Carschooling) turns menial time into meaningful time. While Carschooling is about using ideas and resources to help children and teens learn while on the road, it is also about doing activities that help families spend meaningful time together. With Carschooling, you'll be improving communication, building trust and good will, and bonding your family together in profound and heartfelt ways."*

Diane has over 350 games and activities within her book. Some of the ones she mentions are things like taking pictures of all 50 states of license plates to learn all about the 50 united states, to spotting road signs numbers and saying them in Spanish rather than English, to placing magnetic letters in a shoe box below your child's feet in the car, making a fishing pole out of a stick, a magnet, and a string, and then having your child fish for a letter and having them say a word beginning or ending with that letter and then using it in a sentence.

She also recommends in her book many other books as resources, such as, *Common Birds and Their Songs* by Lang Elliott. This book has photos and information about the birds and comes with companion CD with birdcalls, which is great to take on the road for learning all about birds and then seeing them while driving. And if you are so brave to do so, you can also utilize the learning of the insides of animals and insects, by purchasing for your Life Long Learning road trips, *Skulls and Bones* by Glenn Searfoss. This book explains how scientists examine road kill and skeletal remains of animals and then you can go on your own hunt for remains, such as she suggests, getting plastic baggies and collecting the bugs that splatter in your cars front grill for examination and exploration.

Video Games

Ah, the ever twisting and turning inner turmoil of to video and computer games or not to video and computer games. From my own unique perspective, actually having our boys play video games is actually beneficial in so many ways. There are many logical reasons for and such learning that comes from giving children the gift of having access to video games without placing restrictions upon the quantity of playtime or the type of games played.

Video games provide a **huge** opportunity for learning. I think that it helps to view video games as high quality multimedia demonstrations and interactive, challenging exercises in complex multidisciplinary subject matter. In general, an individual, whether it be a child or an adult, will want to keep playing a video game until they have learned and experienced as much as it is possible for them to learn and experience. Then they stop. It is a bit like reading a novel really. If it is a real page-turner, you do not want to stop in the middle when things are getting exciting, and sometimes you want to read it again right away to understand some of the parts of the book from a new perspective. It is the same thing with video games.

Video games are math as well. That is not just a platitude. Video games really **are** math. Video game strategy and 3D mapping is much higher math than compulsory education can even think of having children learn. Also, through the creation and exploration of various new worlds, children are able to see beyond the box that we as a society tend to place them in, and are able to be out of the box thinkers, thereby, creating unlimitless possibilities for themselves, their lives, and the lives of those around them.

We as humans think and learn best when we attempt to reason via logic and general abstract concepts within perceiving patterns through actual experiences in the world. Video games give to us those patterns within the gaming experience. Video games provide language and symbolic terminology that is a means of learning a whole new language. Video and computer gaming is a language that is viewed by many in our society as wrong and not allowed immersion in, merely because it is in the form of a game. If you were to learn Japanese, you would you not immerse yourself into the language by attempting to read, write, and speak that language? It is the same with video gaming.

What About Learning to Read Within Life Long Learning?

As a former public and private school teacher now a homelearning mom who in the system worked as a reading teacher the last time I was teaching, I can tell you that allowing your child to take the lead on their reading is really the best blessing of unconditional love we can ever gift to our children. As a reading teacher, I was told that I must push the children to read at such and such a level by such and such a grade or time frame. All this did was manifest children whom simply read because they were told to not because they love to read and some children who even hated reading. I can remember that with my own children that when they were your child's age that they had a child like innocence of loving reading and of learning to read. When a child enters the compulsory education system or even with a school-at-home approach (and I know this as I did this with my own children in the whole school-at-home pushing reading and writing and such for several years before coming to the place we are now) this love of learning to read is then quashed by have to's and musts rather than learning naturally.

This forcing of children to read eventually gets them to hate reading and this is why we see so many adults who have been in the schooling environment only read when they have to such as for their jobs. Very few adults read for the sheer pleasure of reading, unless they learned how to step outside of the schooling environment box while in the system. Some like myself, did, others like my husband and my father, hate to read and only read what interests them and very little of that. Reading what interests us, and our children is a wonderful way to learn to read and to love to learn to read, which is why my husband and father in their approach to reading only what they are interested in is ok. It is because they were forced to read as children though that even reading what they are interested in to them becomes a chore and they still do not like it. For an example, my husband would rather listen to a book on CD on something that interests him rather than even consider sitting down with that same material in book format and actually reading it. And this is because he was forced to read as a child that he never had the opportunity to develop his love of reading of his own volition.

Learning naturally does not mean that we do no reading with our child or that they will be free from ever learning how to read, sentence structure and the like. What it does mean is that we allow our child to take the lead, just as the did when they were smaller with picking up a book and reading it. It is seeing too, just like a child first learns the word "Mc Donald's" from that big yellow M in the sky as we drive by, that children learn reading not just from a book but from everywhere and anywhere in life. It really is within learning ourselves that gifting our child with the experience of choosing of their own volition what, when, and how they choose to read that really opens the door for the to WANT to read and to WANT to learn what we call as the "correct way" to spell words and to write them and sentence structure and what is a noun and all of those learnings. And the more they read of their own volition, the more that they will learn about how to read and write and spell. the more that you spend time reading to them and with them so that they see the book, the words, not you just spewing the words out but seeing the written word with you as it is being read or having a second copy of the book if possible so that they can follow what is being spoken with what is being written, the more the will want to learn how it is that we spell, how it is that we write and why words are the way they are.

I myself am testimonial proof of this. Yes, growing up in school I learned about what prepositions were and such. In fact, I got very good at being a robot who memorized the phrase is, are, was, were, am, been, being...and the rest of them I do not remember! Did they help me with reading? Did it help me with writing or spelling? No, because all it was to me was a list of words that I had to memorize for some test. How I did learn to read, write, and spell came from my own love of learning to read. From as far back as I can remember, I would read everything I could get my hands on. Most of my days in school at what we called back then as recess and lunch were spent in the library, reading books. I would beg my mom all the time after school or on weekends to drive me to the library which was only a few blocks from the school I went to as a young child. It was in seeing repeatedly the written word, and taking the time to pronounce it "incorrectly" and then listening to my mom and others in school who were reading to me as I followed along in the same book pointing to each word as it was read to make the association that that sound coming from mom's or other's lips corresponds to this word and this is how it is spelled is what helped me to learn how to read, write, and spell. Other than various members of school teachers reading allowed to me so I could make the correlation, something of which we already provide with our children at home when we read to them as small children, I learned how to read through this manner. Learning through this way provided meaning to the written words, rather than them being jus a bunch of words, I was enjoying the delight of those words as they were within something that I was interested in within merely picking up a book and reading it or being read to. It brought forth my innate curiosity of learning of wanting to learn that all children have and all children do. We are born with an innate sense to learn, it is what we come here to this earth to do. That innate sense of wanting to learn and discover the world around us only gets quashed when we enter the schooling environment and we are told that we have to learn and that the schools way is the only way to learn.

And what about writing and spelling correctly within reading? What if my child never learns how to spell correctly or write correctly or read correctly? I have these questions come to me from parents all the time. My response is that in the gifting of our children choosing of their own volition, we can then realize that learning to write and spelling can come naturally as well because if they are reading of their own volition, then they are able to see that the word 'The' as an example is spelled T H E, right there for them within what they are reading. Then when they come and ask "Hey mommy, how do you spell 'The'?" we can give them the guidance of saying hey lets go look that up in the book you read with that word in it that you were reading the other day, or an hour ago. It is within sharing with the emulation of modeling reading within reading on our own, and reading with our child continuously so that they can see the word being spoken matches the word that is written is what gives life to reading, writing, spelling and to our child wanting to learn these things.

This then also opens the door to offer as a suggestion to play the fun ways of learning things like nouns, verbs, and such and their uses within hands on game like mad libs. Games such as Boggle, or Scrabble, or online Text Twist also help with spelling. If Scrabble is too advanced, then adapt it by just using the letters and allowing your child to create whatever words they can come up with that maybe they have seen in a book they have read or saw on a sign as you were driving to the store. Also we just found a website that I have listed on the Life Long Learning free stuff page called writing backwards. It takes whatever you wish to write and writes it backwards for you. We had a blast for over an hour learning how to spell things backwards and in essence in doing this, the our boys learned the way to spell it "right" as well!. Or like a few weeks back now, we learned to read a whole book backwards! Does you remember the book *Mouse Soup* By Arnold Lobel? It was one of my favorite books as a child that I read and my mom would read to me.

Well, Matthew asked me if I would read it to him the other night and I said sure. Anthony came in during the book and listened to us read as well. So we read it, and afterwards, Matthew asked can we read it backwards? and I said Sure why not? Well what he meant was to read it like as we learned in our learnings of world religions that the Hebrew Bible or Torah is read which is say page 100, then 99, 98, 97, and so on. Well, instead of reading it one page at a time, we ended up reading it backwards one WORD at a time. Thus the sentence the old lady became lady old the, which had Matthew and Anthony and me for that matter busting up laughing. We read all 64 pages of Soup Mouse, of I mean Mouse Soup one sentence at a time backwards! We had a blast! And almost to the beginning or I mean end of the story, Matthew said "Gee Mommy, I never knew reading could be this much fun!" And he is right, what fun it was!! So many times we think that things should be written and said and read in a certain way, but who says? Just because someone years ago said so, does not mean we are not free to learn and explore it in a new way! And in doing so, our boys made a connection to reading, to love of reading, to learning and love of learning that connection that will last a lifetime.

Having fun and playing with words and books, just as you do when your child is small is a wonderful way of learning. Children and (even adults) do learn through play as it takes the 'have to's' out of the equation and makes learning fun! And it you ever doubt whether or not a child is reading, writing, and spelling correctly, then take a look at this ~

I cdnuolt blveiee taht I cluod aulaclty uesdnatnrd waht I was rdanieg. The phaonmneal pweor of the hmuan mnid, aoccdrnig to a rscheearch at Cmabrigde Uinervtisy, it dseno't mtaetr in waht oerdr the ltteres in a wrod are, the olny iproamtnt tihng is taht the frsit and lsat ltteer be in the rghit pclae. The rset can be a taotl mses and you can sitll raed it whotuit a pboerlm. Tihs is bcuseae the huamn mnid deos not raed ervey lteter by istlef, but the wrod as a wlohe. Azanmig huh? yaeh and I awlyas tghuhot slpeling was ipmorantt!

So, yes there are many books that show you how to "teach" your child to read, to write, and to spell. There is many curriculums out there for this. However, I say, that you already have everything you need right there with you already and you have been using it since the day that your child was born, when you began reading to them. There is so much reading available right in our own home or while driving to the grocery store or on a trip to see grandma and grandpa. There is reading on the cereal boxes in the pantry, or of a favorite plaque in your house, or a music CD collection, or video collection in our house. I invite you to just take a look around you to see reading is everywhere. On of the games we love to play the boys and I is to run around the house and see how many things we can find to read. We also sometime do this in the car while driving somewhere. The curriculum then for learning to read is life, life as your curriculum. All you really need are some ideas on how to expand what it is that you are already doing as such a wonderful job of learning with your child the awe-inspiring joy of reading, of writing, and of spelling.

Reading and Math in Video Gaming

Let us explore more in-depth that of learning to read and actually reading within video and computer gaming. In compulsory education, children must learn to read and are given reading tests for comprehension that ask and require general factual, dictionary, and specific cut and dry answers, with no regard to the many facets that the question or questions may have. In many cases as well, children are expected to read and understand words, phases, and sentences that in fact they may not even know of or understand the meaning to, yet they are "required" to know them, simply because the "standards" say they must.

Take for example that of James Paul Gee's (a book I highly recommend reading, as it is pack full of information, much more than I could ever write here about how much we all truly to learn from video gaming) example within his book, *What Video Games Have to Teach Us About Learning and Literacy*, when he states the sentence about basketball ~ *"The guard dribbled down the court, held up two fingers, and passed to the open man"*. James Paul Gee goes on to state that *"A typical reading test would ask a question like this: "What did the guard do to the ball? And give "bounce it" as one of the choices. Unfortunately, you can answer such general, factual, dictionary like questions and really have no idea what the sentence means in the domain of basketball. When we see that the same thing applies to sentences from science or any other schooling type subjects, we immediately see why so many children pass early reading tests but cannot learn later on in other areas of learning subjects".*

Such the same thing can be said about mathematical equations. There are hundreds if not possibly thousands of varieties of ways to conduct the same mathematical equation and yet still come to the same end result answer. In the schooling environment, we begin in the first few years to show this to children, by showing that there are many ways to make the number four, such as that of 2+2, and 3+1 and 5-1 and so on. Yet, somewhere along the way, about the age of nine or ten teachers, administrators, parents, and society as a whole, place a demand upon children to learn a certain way, and are punished if they create another way to solve a mathematical equation that is not the same as the teachers way. I watched this happen time and time again with Chris as he went through 5th and 6th grade. He had one teacher who would literally not count for credit his math schooling work if it was not done exactly the way the teacher had taught it, even when the answers were clearly correct.

By James Paul Gee's example, we can see how children within a schooling environment are placed inside of a box, are "taught", and are only able to view reading and other aspects of learning from one view, rather than being able to step outside of the box and view life and learning from as many sides as possibility allows. Consequently, children today are not learning and are not learning how to think, let alone think out of the box within the schooling environment. They are learning simply how to memorize and recite information as if they are a robot. In the example that James Paul Gee sites, within the context of that one simple sentence, those words can be interpreted in a plethora of ways. We can see that the word dribble for instance, can mean to drool, thereby having a completely diverse meaning from that of a basketball context.

Therefore, if we do not take the time to learn with our children to step out of the box and to view all possibilities of meaning and to see which ones fit within the context of what the author of the words intends and then yet again view it another way still, then our children are missing out on the unlimitless possibilities that life and learning have to offer. They miss the opportunities to take the written word and to translate into something that has meaning and connection to them and to their world.

Video and computer gaming provide this ability to step out of the box. Within any one game, there are literally thousands of ways to read and explore reading in a multitude of contexts, to distinguish and re-distinguish language. There is learning in strategic problem solving, leadership, and that of the journey to achieving total mastery of something. It is that journey to mastery, as well as these other skills and more, that our children can take and utilize their whole life long for learning. And they can do so successfully, much more successfully than that of us or of others before us.

Video and computer gaming also can give us a jumping off point for learning beyond that game. For making connections and experimenting with options for learning within the game and beyond the game. For instance, our boys love the game of *Tetris*. Since *Tetris* is about mathematically stacking sets of blocks together in order to make them fit together into a puzzle dimension to clear levels and of that of patterning, sorting and more, we took this learning and transcended it into that of doing the same thing with *Legos*. *Legos*, then turned into a trip to *Legoland* here in town, where we explored in great detail that of *Legoland Miniland USA*, and also saw an exhibit on how they actually make *Legos*. This turned into history about where Legos came from, which is from Denmark. This turned into an ancestral learning, as my grandmother, the boy's great grandmother, was born, and raised in Copenhagen until the age of two. All of these connections of possibility and more came out of one small video game called *Tetris*. What wonder, what awe, and what learning, and even what fun while we were learning all came from one small video game called *Tetris*.

Matthew and Anthony have also learned so much about how a video game is actually made as well. Matthew took a video game design class in which he learned how to using computer software, design from conception to actually play his own video game. Many mathematical equations and connotations are devised when creating a video game, things of which I cannot even begin to explain, let alone write here within the pages of this book. In the scope of mathematics as a whole, I can honestly say that our children know more high-level math, not only than most children their age, but they know more mathematic skills than that of many adults, including myself and my family!

Matthew has designed several games since that time and has passed on his video game design wisdom to his younger brother Anthony. So not only do our boys have learning from a game playing standpoint, but they also know the "behind the scenes" view, if you will, on what it takes and how much actually goes into the process, frame by frame, of making a video game. Not too many people get this unique perspective, as we usually just view and play with the finished product. Our children have a newfound appreciation for all of the designers and the thousands of hours it takes to produce a game that we can make play and work within mere minutes.

There are a multitude of mathematic equations that can be solved in a myriad of ways in any one video or computer game. And it is not just what society deems as "educational" games that we have out on the market today either. I have observed the mathematical learning of fractions in a game called as *Mario Sunshine*, which is by industry standards not considered an "educational game", yet there is much learning within the dimensions of this game and all of the thousands upon thousand of gaming options available today.

I often sit and laugh when hearing the words spoken by others when they call something educational, or that a game or toy is educational. I laugh because the notion that only certain select things are considered "educational" to me sound to be rather absurd. Everything in life has something of value to learn from, from the speck of dirt on someone shoe all the way through to the concept of what planets exist in our universe, and everything in between. We can learn from anything and everything that life and all that is in life, has to offer us. So to say that only certain things are educational and others are not, seems rather silly to me.

For the Love of the Game

I tend to view our children's video gaming as their work or their passion ~ work that they are immersed in and love. And there is such a love for it that it does not feel like work to them at all. Kind of like in life for us as adults, when we find our life's passion or purpose, we love what we do, and we do what we love.

Is that not that what we want for our children? This is not mere "fun" or just a passive form of entertainment; this is something that is complex and full of learning in all aspects of life. I watch our children with some of these games and I am literally amazed at their incredible capacity and ability of learning such complex, intrinsic games. And just like that life's passion that we as adults find, they do not want to be pulled away from it, just as we do not. Like anyone else's work that they love, they continue thinking about it, even when they are away from it.

I have seen our children get very frustrated with a game, walk away from it, let it sit in their minds for awhile, and then return to it with a new strategy, a new perspective, and be able to do what they could not do earlier. That is satisfying work. That is confronting a challenge instead of running away from it. Speaking of challenges ~ this is one thing that I love observing in our boys, is that I notice the perseverance and determination they have ~ how they do not shy away from the challenge of the game that they love. It seems that the more and more challenging the video game gets, the more determined they are and the more they keep coming back, trusting they will learn and expand with the game.

I have watched this many a times with our boys. Anthony will be playing a *Nintendo 64* game called *Starfox*, and he will at times become frustrated over not being able to move forward to the next level. He will shut it off for a while, come back to it later, only to find that he was able to unlock some portal within the game and has not only moved on past the level he did not before, but two or three other levels besides!

When it is a new game, our boys want to be playing it as much as possible. It becomes the immersion of learning process that I described in detail back in chapter two all over again. It is that wonder, that awe, which is what makes Life Long Learning such a blessed family connecting and bonding experience, no matter what type of family you have.

Suggestions to Expand the Video Gaming Experience

So, what to do if your child or children have a love affair with learning within the video and computer gaming genres? The same thing that you would do with whatever passion your child or children wishes to take on in their lives of learning ~ Watch them play. Join their play. Bring them treats and lunch. Talk about the game. Ask questions about the game. Talk to them about their games, about the aspects that captivate them the most, getting the view from, and being in "their world with them". By joining them in their world, you are building a bond with them and learning to see what the world looks like through their eyes.

You can even learn about the history of video gaming together. PBS has a wonderful website dedicated to the history of video gaming. It is available at the time of the writing of this book at http://www.pbs.org/kcts/videogamerevolution/. Our boys surely loved doing this together with me. They even have a quiz of sounds to see if you can guess which video gaming sound goes to which game. We got most of them right too! All but two I think if I remember. We spent quite a few hours bonding while reading, and my reminiscing with them about how the video games used to be when they first came out when I was growing up, and how far they have come in the gaming industry. Of course, Matthew and Anthony could not believe that mom was **that** old to have ever played the very first invented video games, but hey!

When your child(ren) have had their fill and they are ready to see what the rest of the world has to offer, you will have formed a valuable connection, and you can talk about their game with them and with others as well. Your child(ren) also will tend to be more open to something you want to suggest to do together, because it will not seem like you are just trying to get them away from the game or that you have not taken an interest in what they are learning and only doing what it is that you want to do. It will seem like you genuinely just want to spend time with them doing something great, because you have given them the gift of showing them that you do care about them, what they are learning, and what their passions and interests are.

Other ideas for making the video gaming experience more exciting still might be to buy them video game hint magazines for their games. Help them find web sites that give cheat codes and hints for their games. Invite friends over who like to play the same games with them that they do and make a video gaming party. Or maybe they might be interested in doing a project on something related to their favorite game. Eventually your child(ren) do have their fill of the games and believe me, they will. At some point they do stop playing of their own volition, or at least start taking longer and longer breaks in between. And in between that time, enjoy the wonder of learning with them all of the games that you can, because in the game that we call life here on this earth, it is one of the most fun ways to learn!

~

If you change the way you look at things; the things you look at will change ~ Wayne Dyer

Chapter Ten

Sweet Dreams ~ Our Own Intuitive Clocks

One of the best things that I have found is that as a Life Long Learning family we really have time together. Hours upon hours where we can sit and talk and really get to know each other, love each other, and really just **BE** a family, without so much of the stress of running around and trying to be "doing" things or going here and there in a rush all the time, as we were when they were in the schooling environment. We have more time to really enjoy each other, and enjoy life. Rather than the boys just "tolerating " each other simply because they are blood related and live in the same house, they have bonded as brothers.

One of my most endearing *Mommy Moments* came the first night our boys all "camped" out together in Chris's room. I can remember it being so sweet that of course being the *Mommy Moment* that it was, it made me cry. I can remember one night about 11:30 in the evening, being in my room here, typing away at an email to a friend, when I heard Matthew say to Anthony, "Hey let's go sleep in Chris's room" and Anthony then saying "Yeah! Let's ask him if we can". I remember hearing the pitter patter of their feet like reindeer hooves on the roof on Christmas Eve, pounding up the stairs and into Chris's room.

Listening intently, the next thing I hear is Chris saying "Sure guys, let's do a movie and show night and we will curl up together and watch some shows before we go to bed". Of course, by then, I had just stopped emailing my friend and was just sitting in my room teary-eyed listening to this with my heart so filled with love and joy.

Just then, I was startled when Anthony and Mathew came running into my room, so I had to make it look like I was still writing my email and they both said "Mommy, we are going to sleep in Chris's room tonight, and we are going to get our blankets and pillows, ok, Mommy, we love you, good night" as they ran back out the door. I called back to them, "Ok, just don't forget to brush your teeth and go to the bathroom!" A few moments later, Chris comes in and says to me "Yeah, I told them it was ok, we are going to hang out together and watch shows and stuff". To which I said "Ok, honey, you are an awesome big brother, thanks! I love you!"

And so it went that this was their first night of many nights of sleeping in the same room together. Of course, they each still have their own rooms, their own sanctuary, for those times when they get on each other's last nerve, to be able to have a place to have some time to themselves if they choose. However, those times are few and far between because they have learned how to be in sync with each other, living together day by day, all day everyday.

"Schooling" Siblings

The biggest reason that children who are in the schooling environment have such a hard time getting along with their siblings is because they have never really had time to be with their brothers or sisters for any extended length of time. Sure, they may have holiday breaks or summer vacation, however, often times, summer vacation is now down to eight weeks compared to that of what it was when I was in school of almost fourteen weeks. Those eight weeks of summer school is usually filled with similar "schooled" like activities such as camps and classes, most of them not of the child's choice. Those eight weeks are never really a vacation per se, and certainly is not enough time to get to know the idiosyncrasies and rhythms of each other that living together day in and day out provides.

Holiday break certainly is not the appropriate time for forging bonding relationships for children in the schooling environment either. The stress of the holidays, having parents who are stressed about the holidays, family and friends in and out of town, and having each child having to make sure their book report or other schooling assignment is complete before the two weeks are up, does not make a conducive environment for brotherly or sisterly connections.

If there is any form of bonding in that shorten period of time, it is quite that, shortened. Short lived due to the fact that once school resumes for these children, it is back to square one. The cycle begins all over again as to how they cannot relate to their sibling simply because they are not given ample time and space to be around them constantly to learn how to relate to them on a continuous basis. Each of them considers the other as the person whom I call my brother or sister but all I really do is I share a ride to school with them, say hello briefly to before I have to be up in my room doing homework for hours on end, maybe get to talk to briefly at dinner if we all get to eat at the same time, and say good night to before going to sleep, only to get up and do it all over again the next day.

Oh, and then there are the weekends during the "school" year! The weekends filled with the competitive sports, and rehearsals, the drive here and drive there if that is not also being done during the week as well. The children within the compulsory educational environment get to spend so much time bonding with their siblings fighting in the car about who gets the back seat and who is going to be late to their game because Susie took too long in the bathroom combing her hair this morning!

Let us not also forget the things that are "taught" in school of which they bring home with them, as well. The "You cannot play with me because you are not my age, have my interest, or the fact that simply because you are my sibling"; or the bullying aspect of "I am bigger and better than you, therefore, I will boss you around, make fun of you, and treat you like nothing". Is it any wonder then why children whom are in the schooling environment have no really concept of what it is like to be a brother or sister to their sibling!

Musical Rooms

I have thoroughly enjoyed the fact that when the boys are all camping together in Chris's room, that they do not get sick of each other in the way that most schooled children do of there siblings within being together for more than one hour at a time. Now do not get me wrong, do they still have their little tiffs with each other? You bet they do. None of our children are perfect little angels all of the time. They still have their moments of "Mom, he did this to me" or "Mom, he won't let me have the game piece" etc. However, I have to say on a whole, it does happen less frequently, much less frequently then it did when we were in the schooling environment.

It is so enjoyable every night as I sit here in bed reading or writing, to listen to the sounds of their laughter ~ of them playing together in Chris's room, of them talking and tickling each other and on occasion, hearing them come bursting out of the room running from each other in laughter over some silly game they were playing under the bed that they ended up chasing each other. There is a peace, a love, and a true bonding in its rarest of forms between our boys. There is a peace and happiness in my heart, a love for our boys, and a love of life. This is one of the true essences of Life Long Learning.

It has been interesting too, how as time has gone on how Chris, Matthew, and Anthony will play musical rooms. Some nights they will all come camp out in our room, as in the one night when the electricity went out. Or they will sleep in Matthew's room, such as one morning, I woke up and went downstairs only to find Matthew and Anthony curled up in Matthew's twin bed snuggled up tight together. I had tried to get a picture but by the time I went to go get the camera, Matthew had woken up, darn it!

Other nights too, one of the boys will sleep in our room, and two in another of the boy's rooms, and even still there are other nights where we will all sleep in the living room together, or the boys will make a tent in the living room and sleep. One night Matthew and Anthony did this where they made a tent, complete with our portable T.V., snacks, and drinks and hung out all night until finally crashing out to sleep about 4 a.m.

Time for Bed?

Just as with pretty much everything in Life Long Learning, or in that of life, we "deschooled" bedtimes as well. Simply put, our children just like us, go to bed when we are sleepy and when our body says that it is time to rest, not when someone imposes a particular time to go to sleep.

In the Life Long Learning philosophy, to insist that your children be in their rooms by a certain time each night or that they be banished to their rooms after a certain time, as if they were on room arrest, regardless of their wills, desires, or plans for the evening, is not respectful of our children as people. Treating children as second class citizens subject to our whims is as if we consider them to be subservient members to the family, of which they are not, nor never should be. Our children are apart of our family, not subservient members to the family.

Also stating that you "insist" in the first place implies that you have some leverage you are using in order to bend them to your will. Think of how we would feel if someone came to us at 8:30 in the evening clicked off the T.V. and then stood in front of the T.V. and said "Ok, you must now go to bed". We would be angry and insulted that we are not given the choice as to when we feel we are ready for sleep. Yet this is often exactly what we do to our children.

But, Don't We Know What is Best for Our Children?

While it may be true that there are times in which we may feel we know what is best for our children, I am here to say that in most cases, we indeed do not as we think we do. While we may know that it is best for our children to look both ways when crossing the street, and we will guide them to do so, so that they do not get ran over by a car, the choice of when their bodies need sleep is something that is only known by each individual themselves. Who but you, or but each of our children, knows better than we when their bodies are in need of sleep but them?!

We are not inside our children's bodies; we cannot control what their own intuitive clock is saying the "right" time for bed! Only they can do this. Only we have control over our bodies own intuitive response to sleep.

It is like when we go to a doctor and they attempt to rate our condition based upon symptoms in a book that say we have such and such ailment and that we must have such and such symptoms, but we do not have symptom A we have symptom B. Who knows our body better than we do? Our doctors, simply because they have a medical degree or a medical book that says so? That we should believe that doctor and that book over what we know in our body to be true? I should say not. Our body is our best guide, rather than a doctor's degree or book that says so!

Yes, we can definitely see the signs of tiredness, such as the preverbal rubbing of the eyes, or the crankiness (although can also be a sign for other things such as hunger or boredom or something that happened that they are upset about) or the droopy eyes. At that point, we can as I often do, ask for them to come curl up with me to read a story, or watch a show, or just to cuddle and talk. But to insist on them being banished to their rooms turns their room, which is to be a place of love, refuge, and serenity, into a battle ground, a place they come to hate going to, and often makes sleep an unpleasant thing that they do not wish to do because sleep is then seen as a punishment.

Our children embrace and enjoy sleep as a time to revitalize their bodies and to allow their minds to rest so that their bodies and spirits can grow. They find solace and contentment in their rooms as in all of the rooms in the house are because their room is a peaceful place to sleep in and rejuvenate in.

What About the Importance Routines?

"But!" you are saying, "We have a routine, and our children know the routine and if we veer from it……..

I used to be the *"Queen of Routine"* when our boys were within the schooling environment. Being the teacher I was constantly having to schedule increments of "schooled" learning and "learning by the bell" with a chart for every hour of the "school" day. I had every nook and cranny of their lives down to a science. We would come home from school and I would go through each of their backpacks, go over what went on during the day at school, and what was for homework. Then they would have one to two hours of "unstructured" playtime, and then it would be time to have dinner by no later than six, which meant I had to stress about getting everything started by five at least! Then immediately after dinner it was straight to homework, which usually lasted for Matthew and Anthony until 8 p.m. (if there was no arguing over homework as I usually had every night with Matthew) and Chris well past that so his "bedtime" was always later. At eight, Matthew and Anthony **had** to read, brush teeth, be in "bed" with the door closed and the timer on the T.V. for a show for only 30 minutes so they would be asleep by no later than nine. There would be groundings or toys taken away for not being asleep by nine. Of course we would all be up by between 6 a.m. and 6:30 a.m. to do it **all** over again! Whew! I am stressed out and tired all over again, just writing all of that out that we used to have to do everyday.

Now, this is not to say that as a Life Long Learning family that we do not have routines. You bet we still do. We do still have routines, however, they are not parent imposed routines. They are more what I would call traditional everyday things that we do. They do not have to be done in any particular order per se, but we still do them. We still do laundry everyday and the dishwasher too. We still clean our rooms on average once a week and we still vacuum the rugs.

We all still brush our teeth and go to the bathroom before sleep, whether that be at 10 p.m. or 4:30 a.m. We all still have our own way of winding down before sleep. Me, I often read or write before I go to sleep. Aaron, he usually zones out in front of the T.V. for a while or plays with his Yu-Gi-Oh cards and duels the boys. Chris, Matthew, and Anthony, each have their own ways of winding down separately at times with Matthew likes to do sketching and Anthony counting and placing his Yu-Gi-Oh, Pokemon, Football, or Baseball cards in his folders or making his own book. Chris likes to tinker with his computer before winding down to bed. Other times it is a good old fashioned wrestling match on our bed to run off the last bit of energy before winding down to sleep.

There is no more "grounding", for not going to "bed" on time or having any of those fights and battles over all of that, making the house tense right before sleep. There is a peace that comes over the house at night now, a serenity that is surreal. We as a family at times will meditate to ground and center ourselves, so if there is any grounding to do, it will be that type of grounding that goes on in our home at night, not the *other* type of grounding. The boys often tease Aaron and I before we say we are turning in for the night, asking us "Aren't you going to *ground* us before you go to sleep Mom and Dad?" wanting to know if we are going to meditate together that night or not.

There too, are times when collectively the three of them or all of us as a family, will play a board game or a video game or watch a show together before going to sleep. The different things that they like to do for that space of time before bed may be different each night, but all of us have that traditional everyday time where we do some of what would be called a "routine" by most people before going to sleep.

If the boys are still playing or watching a show or doing something else when we are ready to crash, we tell them we are headed to bed and if they want to have some cuddle time or a story with us that they better come get it while they can, or we will be asleep. Sometimes they choose to get a story or two while the getting is good and then go back to whatever it was that they were doing before we started having our time together. Sometimes they choose to forgo the cuddle time and finish their movie, or whatever they are involved in at that time.

Sometimes it is the same time we all go to sleep, occasionally they fall asleep earlier than we do because they are tired and had a busy day with friends over or a project that they worked on that was particularly energy zapping, and yet sometimes they stay up later than we do. They usually do not stay up long after we are in bed, in fact there are still many nights I am the one who is up the latest, especially now writing this book. There will be times yet, when I think they are all asleep as I am up writing and then Matthew will come in and want to have his special cuddle time with me then, when the house is quiet. I love those times when we cuddle like that when the house is quiet and it is like it is just us because it feels as if the whole world but us is asleep. We talk about life and about whatever he wants to talk about. It is our one on one bonding time that I so cherish and I know he does too.

Routines are fine, children often find it comforting to know what comes next, and a routine can help even many adults wind their minds down for sleep. However, when a routine becomes our own imposed routine upon others, which includes the threat of not getting certain things such as the special time for story with you if they fails to toe the line, that does not seem like a very inviting routine to me.

As a Life Long Learning family, we do not sweat the small stuff. Just as in everything in Life Long Learning, they will learn how and when their "routine" is and what it will look like to them each and every night on their own and in their own way. The point in sharing this chapter with you is that it is their choice. We get our needs met by going to bed when we need to, and they go to bed when they need to.

Our Own Intuitive Clocks

One of the intriguing aspects of Life Long Learning that goes hand in hand with that of going to sleep when one is naturally ready is that of honoring our own intuitive clock. As a Life Long Learner, being free from space and time restrictions seems to become a natural state of being.

All of us here in our home are living our lives by our own intuitive clocks. We do not wear watches, with the exceptions when it is rather important to know the time, say if we have to be at a friend's house at two in the afternoon or if my husband has to be at a meeting for work by nine a.m. There are days if it were not for the clock on my computer, I would not know the time. Our bodies our lives are becoming less and less in tune with the time clock and more on what our body's needs and that of our minds wish to be focused on. Being on our own intuitive clock also means that there is no time constraints to learning, as far as what our children are supposedly to learn and by when or how.

I have heard information from many sources that right now quantum physicists are experimenting with the issues of time. It is believed that in the not so distant future those scientists will discover evidence that will change how humans view time. Scientists will show that humans obsession with timepieces and calendars are actually limiting and restricting us and our learning on many different levels of consciousness. By constantly checking our watches and calendars, we are denying our ability to be learning in many modalities simultaneously. Therefore the belief in this concept that we created, that we know as time and space restrictions, is what is causing us to be limited in our learning.

Is not true that as a society, that we allow the measurement upon our wrist and upon our walls to rule us? Do we not expend great amounts of energy, trying to keep up with an incessant ticking of a clock, thinking that we are going to run out of something that we can never run out of? And yet, we do not acknowledge that while the clock is never ending, that our human bodies need to stop and rest.

We are constantly in competition with a time machine that only exists because we say it exists because someone created it and said it was so. We rush along, flying through life, never really noticing all of the beauty in this life that we are missing. We often spin our lives as fast as the sweeping second hand, chasing the seconds.

Are we able to learn and create in this mindset? No. We are not able to create when we are under pressure. I believe it was Einstein who said, *"Necessity is the mother of invention"*. I rather believe that this quote should say that of *"Choice is the mother of invention and creation"*. However, in no where does Einstein say that time and that of racing the clock is.

This is why children of compulsory education cannot learn, as they are always under pressure to learn now, now, now. They are never able to rest their minds in a calmer state then that of fast pace so that they can learn. This too, is why people in our society are so unproductive in their jobs and careers. They are not given the ability to take as long as they need to allow the ideas and creations from within them to flow. The boss always wants the work done right now. Why this rush? We have our whole lives to create, to learn. It is not until we stop mimicking a timepiece as if it owns us, when our mind has been slowed to a more restful and calmed state that we are able to give birth to new ideas and where learning can take place.

Therefore, in the not so distant future we will discover that once remove this belief that we will be awakening to our own inner intuitive clocks in place of the time clocks and calendars that we know now. That in doing so will awaken us to the unlimitless possibilities and regain our own natural talents and abilities in life. It is going to take us doing it one family at a time, but it will occur. With Life Long Learning, you too can open up that world of limitless possibilities.

~

What we have to learn to do, we learn by doing
~ Aristotle (384-322 BC), Greek philosopher

Chapter Eleven

I Am a Social Butterfly – Life Long Learning and Socialization

We have come to the point in the book where, by now, you should be feeling rather confident in the fact that, yes, your family is a Life Long Learning family. That yes, learning comes about in all forms, shapes, and sizes. You have (hopefully!) even made it through "the talk" with the family on your learning approach with your children and how they may or may not agree with it all. And here *you thought* that "the talk" was the talk about sex, you know, those "birds and bees" talk that you have with your children when they get to be "that age" all these years!

So now, Ah! The sixty-four million dollar questions of the new millennium is now asked (and answered!) within the pages of this chapter, which is......

If we are a Life Long Learning family, how will I ever be sure that my children are well "socialized"? How do I know that they will be able to get along in society if they have never been around people their own age to relate with?

Even though I am not fond of definitions, per se, as this and labels, tend to place people and things, and life into a box that need to be conformed to (which I will speak of more in depth in the next chapter!), let's take a look for a moment at the word socialization and what it means. Upon looking the word up in the dictionary, these are the definitions I found....

1. *To place under government or group ownership or control.*

2. *To make fit for companionship with others; make sociable.*

3. *To convert or adapt to the needs of society.*

Now, given these definitions, this begs the question ~ Is this **really** what we wish to do to our children? Is this **really** what we wish to subject them to? Yet, this is exactly what we do each day we take our child and "ship" them off to that institutional setting that we call in today's society as school.

I do not know about you, but I do not wish to place our children under any type of government ownership or control. I certainly do not wish to make our children "fit in" for companionship with others. Nor do I wish to subject our children to having to be "converted" to the needs of society!

My fondest and dearest wish is that our children make friends with others in whatever manner they wish to, to make the connections of their choosing, not because they were placed in a position to where they must be friends with someone simply because their last name begins with the same letter as theirs does. Or because the government says that they have to because they are all seven and therefore are "second graders".

Being Placed in Groups

Think back a bit to when you were in the schooling experience. Now think of how many other children you were "forced" to be friends with because their last name began with the same letter as yours, or because you were in the same reading group, or because you simply were in the same class together. Now when you continue to hold this picture within your mind, ask yourself, how many of them are you friends with today? How many children you spent in some cases as many as twelve years plus of school with, are still your friends today?

Here are a few pieces of information that you might find interesting. My husband Aaron, keep in touch regularly with one friend, I keep in touch occasionally with one friend from my schooling experience. My parents, my father had one, which has since crossed over, and my mother none that I am aware of. Her three best friends she does keep in touch with, were and are her best friends, were so because they lived on the same block and yes, they did go to school together for a time, but their main reason for their initial friendship, had nothing whatsoever to do with compulsory education.

I could go on and on. So I ask you to take a look around you, ask a around of your friends currently and of your family. Make it like a research poll that maybe your children may or may not wish to participate in the learning of how to conduct a survey. See how many people are still friends with the people they went to school with and how many. I will bet you from that small survey you will find the same or similar results that I did.

The reason that these "friendships" within the schooling environment cease to exist after school is out of the picture, is simply the fact that we no longer have "school" in common. Whereby, the friendships were based upon the fact that we were in "fourth grade" together or knew the same people in school, is not a means to *stay* together as friends once the schooling experience has ended. The commonality is then gone, and if you do not have anything in common with another, then where is a basis for the friendship.

Age as a Basis for Commonality

So, one could argue, stating that "Schools are well intentioned though, as they group children together by age, thereby giving them a bond of commonality". This is quite true, they do this. However well intentioned it may be, what tends to happen is that this form of commonality without any other commonalities such as that of common interests and activities, common family backgrounds, common passions, and common like's and dislikes, children then end up being "excluded" from the group based upon those other commonalities that within the group of say, "third graders" in a schooling environment as an example, will generate.

This is where the concept of bullying comes in. What tends to happen is, (in this true to life example above of third graders that also exists on other "grade levels") the only thing that these third graders have in common is that they have been told that they must be together because of the fact that they are all eight years of age, these children will begin to see that this will not be the glue that holds them together in friendships. So in order to "survive" the schooling experience, children will actively seek out other forms of connection to other children. They also do so because as I spoke of before, one of the best modalities we learn through is by that of making connections, not just to things in life, but to people as well.

Upon making these commonality connections, it is then discovered, invariably, that one or more of the children does not share the same interest, hair color, shoes etc. Thereby, one group of children develops the mentality I spoke of previously in chapter two, which is "I am or we are better than you are!" Thus, this child or group will in turn "bully" their way around the ones who do not "fit in" to attempt to keep their status of "I am better than you" and also to make themselves feel better for not "fitting in" elsewhere. This then, is where our life long cycle of "exclusiveness" comes from.

People will often use the bully as an example of why it is so important to let children "socialize" at school. If that is so important, then the bully needs to go to prison after a few months, because society simply does not put up with this bullying type of behavior within life after school, as this person in society is arrested for what is known as assault and battery. So if as adults in mainstream society do not have to put up with this type of behavior, then why should any child be made to put up with it just because they are in school?

Yes, there are adults who do things that are not what we term in society as correct or proper behavior, but we currently have laws that are there for the purpose of taking care of such things. Do our children within compulsory education? Yes and no. Yes, there may be better "rules" however, if a child being bullied is too scared to speak up for fear of retaliation, then what good do these "rules" do? In truth, we as adults have the choice to walk away or leave a situation of this nature. Our children within the schooling environment are not given that freedom or that choice. If fact, if they do attempt to exercise that choice within the system, they are often punished for it, meanwhile the bully gets off "scott free" as they say. Or worse as they may have to suffer the fate of further mistreatment from the bully in question.

Others would argue still that these children being picked on should just "toughen up". Personally, I would never expect my children to put up with bad treatment from a bully in the name of "toughening them up." For what? So they can be submissive to others who treat them in this manner when they grow up too? So they can "ignore" their miserable bosses and abusive spouses? In real life, if an employer discovers that an employee was harassing the other staff members, that employee could be suspended or fired pending an investigation and evaluation or relocated. In real life, if you are so dreadfully harassed by a coworker you can seek legal recourse independently. In a classroom setting, the teacher and other children are often powerless.

The Exception to the "Rule"

Now, in some cases, you will find exceptions to the supposed "rule" regarding the children whom do indeed stay friends, and often times, close friends, regardless of the fact that the only thing they had in common is the same classroom while in school. The children who seek and find the commonalities among them that exist outside of the classroom or schooling setting, tend to be those few exceptions to the rule of you only have friends in school and that those friendship go by the weigh side once you leave school. If children within the schooling environment can relate to each other outside with other related activities, interests, family backgrounds etc. then there may be a basis for a lifetime friendship should these children choose to.

In those cases where the friendship did endure, you are more than likely liable to find the same experience over and over again ~ which is that their friendship did survive due to their outside the box creativity and ingenuity both in out of school interests, and that of what I affectionately call "inside school sneakiness".

Now, go back to that vision you earlier had with the friends you had or did not have with the institutional setting. Remember now the friends you did have while you were there. Now remember how may times you got into trouble, calls home from the teachers or principles, and/or how many times in your report card was it written "talks to much in class". Or how many times were you told by teachers and administrators, "This is not a social hour children". Even though we were as children "grouped" into commonalities, "socialization" was never and is not ever now really encouraged within compulsory education. In fact children then as they do now, get punished for trying to forge friendships to begin with!

Now I ask you, is this *really* socialization as it is meant to be in terms of making and keeping friendships based upon commonalities as we are told our children supposedly receive while in the schooling environment?

What Does Age Got to do with it?
The Old and the Beautiful

So, in the manner that *Tina Turner's* song conveys, I ask *"What does age got to do with it?"* Really. When we "grow up", leave school, and move out on our own, do we really only associate with, converse with, relate with, and form friendships with people who are our own age? I should say not. I have friends that range from the littlest of babies all the way up to eighty-five years old! As do our children. In fact, two of Chris's closets friends, that he both admirers and has much in common with, are in their sixty's. These two women have taken on the role of his guides in many ways in his life, as well as, given Chris the opportunity to guide them. He has learned just as much from these wonderful women as they have from him. He considers them both to be his mentors in many ways.

I remember growing up being a bit uncomfortable around what we as children called "old people". Although I had my grandmother and my great aunt taking care of me a lot during my younger years when my parents would go out to eat or on vacations, I felt often uncomfortable around the senior generation as a child simply because of the fact that the schooling environment "taught" me that although elders were to be respected, that they were also only there to "teach" us and not to be our friends, as their was no way we could be friends with anyone who was not of our "age".

As a person wrote in the following in an article (the author is unknown as of the publication of this book) stated, "*…I have never felt it would be beneficial to stick my six year old in a room full of other six year olds. I believe that the world was created full of people of all ages and sexes to insure that the younger ones and older ones learned from each other. A few years ago, we were living thousands of miles from any older family members, so I brought my children (then five and two) to an assisted living facility, so they could interact with the elderly. Staff members told us that many of the older people would wake up every day and ask if we would be visiting soon. We always went on Wednesdays. My daughters learned some old show tunes while one of the men played piano, and the others would sing along. If a friend were too sick to come out of their room during our visit, we would often spend a few minutes in their room. I always let them give the children whatever cookies they had baked for them, and I ended up cleaning a few of the apartments while we visited, simply because I would have done the same for my own Grandmother. Every room had pictures from my children posted on their refrigerators. We called this "Visiting the Grandmas and Grandpas" and my daughters both (almost two years later) have fond memories of our visits. I am sure that if we were still visiting there, my unborn child would have a thousand handmade blankets and booties to keep him warm all winter. I do not remember any* *such experiences in my entire school life, although I do remember being a bit afraid of old people if they were too wrinkly or weak looking. I never really knew anyone over sixty. I never sped down the hall on someone's wheelchair lap, squealing as we popped wheelies and screeched around corners. I never got to hear stories about what life was like before indoor plumbing and electricity, from the point of view of a woman with Alzheimer's, who might believe she was still five years old, talking with my daughter as if she were a friend. I never got to help a ninety year. old woman keep her arm steady while she painted a picture. And I never watched a room full of "grandma's" waiting for me by the window, because we were fifteen minutes late."*

Missing out?

Given this in-depth look into what school really does to "socialize" our children, and if, as teachers and administrators so say that schools are not made for socializing, then why on earth would anyone assume that our children being within a Life Long Learning modality be missing out on "socialization"?

I refer again to the article that was written by an unknown author that states the following "*.....As a society full of people whose childhood's were spent waiting anxiously for recess time, and trying desperately to "socialize" with the children in class; It is often difficult for people to have an image of a child whose social life is NOT based on school buddies. Do you ever remember sitting in class, and wanting desperately to speak to your friend? It is kind of hard to concentrate on the lessons when you are bouncing around trying not to talk. Have you ever had a teacher who rearranged the seats every now and then, to prevent talking, splitting up friends, and "talking corners?" Were you ever caught passing notes in class? Now ~ flash forward to "real life." Imagine the following scenes:*

Your employer is auditing their interoffice e-mail system and comes across a personal note between you and a coworker. You are required to stand at the podium in the next sales meeting to read it aloud to your coworkers. The Police knock on your door, and announce that because you and your neighbor have gotten so close, they're separating you. You must move your home and your belongings to the other side of town, and you may only meet at public places on weekends.

You are sitting at a booth waiting for a coworker to arrive for a scheduled lunch date. Suddenly a member of upper management sits down across from you and demands your credit cards. When your friend arrives, you just order water and claim you are not hungry, since he stole your lunch money.

You are applying for a job and in an unconventional hiring practice; you are made to line up with other applicants, and wait patiently while representatives from two competing companies take their pick from the lineup.

You are taking your parents out for an anniversary dinner. After you find a table, a waiter tells you that seniors have a separate dining room, lest they "corrupt" the younger members of society.

You go to the grocery store only to find that since you are thirty-two years old you must shop at the store for thirty-two year olds. It is eight miles away and they do not sell meat because the manager is a vegetarian, but your birthday is coming up and soon you will be able to shop at the store for thirty-three year olds.

You would like to learn about Aviation History. You go to the library and check out a book on the subject only to be given a list of "other subjects" that you must read about before you are permitted to check out the aviation book.

You are having a hard time finding what you need in the local department store. The sales clerk explains that each item is arranged alphabetically in the store, so instead of having a section for shoes, you will find the men's shoes in between the maternity clothes and the mirrors.

Your Cable Company announces that anyone wishing to watch the Superbowl this year must log on a certain number of hours watching the Discovery Channel before they can be permitted to watch the game.

You apply for a job only to be told that this job is for twenty-nine year olds. Since you are thirty-two, you will have to stay with your level.

In a group project, your boss decides to pair you up with the person you do not "click" with. His hope is that you will get learn to get along with each other, regardless of how the project turns out. "

Does this really happen in real life outside of compulsory education? No. However, if we were to see school as real life, then this is very well what could be if we were to apply the realities of the schooling environment to what happens outside of institutional learning. All of this leads me to feel quite confident in the wisdom that our children really are not missing out on any social skills being supposedly "taught" in school.

Social Skills within the Life Long Learning Modality

As a Life Long Learning family, the first place we learn how to relate with and forge friendships with others begins right with our family. As I have written throughout this book, being able to **be** together as a family unit on a consistent basis automatically gives us the social skills on how to relate to others, as we know quite intimately, how to be a close family. That is not to say that other families are not close, it is just that we have learned to be close in a way free from the forced misconceptions of the compulsory educational environment.

From there, we branch out. As Life Long Learners, just as anyone living life, we interact daily with people of all ages, sexes, and backgrounds. We talk to and learn from everyone who strikes our interest. We do not limit ourselves to only seeking out opportunities to know people based solely upon our age, sex, or background. Commonalities are important for lasting friendships; however, we can and do relate to or socialize with others regardless if they are or become our life long friends. Whether we mingle with our mail lady when getting our mail, with the grocery clerk at the store, with the man who owns the local card shop, to the mom walking her baby in a baby carriage while we are on a walk by our local creek, we are continuously relating to and learning from people, thereby our children are socializing and are having learning opportunities for learning within these interactions constantly.

All three of our boys have developed a wonderful friendship with a man who owns a local card shop. Through the boys' love of Yu-Gi-Oh cards, baseball card, and other card, they have learned so much from this forty something man. He has taken Matthew under his wing as a mentor of sorts, in encouraging Matthew in his developing of his own card game, as well as helping our boys to learn all about the history of many card games available out there today. His vast knowledge and wisdom of cards has been information and a bond that our boys will treasure always. As of the writing of this book, we have learned that he is going to be selling his card shop and retiring to the eastern coast of the US to be with his family. So, Mike, we will miss you, and thank you for all you have done for us. The gift of knowledge and of love you have given to us has been priceless.

Manners and the 'D' Word

Where did we, as children, learn our manners from? I do not know about you but, I learned how to treat others well from my family at home. Certainly not from the school system! Learning manners is a part of socializing. It is the way of relating to others that shows that we value and respect another person, irregardless of their age, sex, or background. How else will a child learn to hold a door for a woman, or not to ask a woman her age, if we do not model these items while our children are actually around us to see them? If they are at school or have their nose in a book memorizing facts that have no meaning to them or their lives, they certainly will not be able to.

Modeling, I believe is the key to children, to anyone learning manners. You can tell someone (in particular a child) until you are blue in the face not to pick their nose in public, and yet if you are modeling picking your nose secretly and they catch you, then that hour you spent literally lecturing them on why it is not considered in society as appropriate has no value. Add that to the natural innate curiosity of a child, and this is why parents often find themselves in fights over how to "discipline" a child.

You know the word discipline, refers to the word "disciple" which means follower, or to follow. I do not know about you, but I believe we have way too many "followers" in this world. Individuals and children who "follow" simply because they are told too, are like robots, and personally, I do not wish for any of our children to be a mind-less robot, unless it is of their choosing. I wish if they choose to be a follower that it be because they have researched the information available out there to them, then searched their hearts and souls for what they truly believe is what works for them and then forging forward as a leader with a group because they choose to, rather than just be a mind-less follower. Not to mention given the freedom and choice, most people who sheepishly do follow, if they were not going to be ridiculed or teased by others for doing so, would jump at the chance to be a leader.

Thus modeling, whether it is manners, or any form of learning, is an excellent Life Long Learning gift and social gift to learn and utilize. I believe that manners are not these skills to be "learned" per se, but rather a gift of love that we give to our children and to others within this earth. It is a way of honoring the person that they are.

Now of course this does not completely guarantee that if you model a certain gift that you wish for your children to adopt, that they necessarily will do so. But the option is now there, as the exposure of such a possibility exists now because you placed that possibility into existence by showing, or modeling it. We model and use manners in our home. And a sense of love comes over me every time when we go out, that one of our boys holds a door open for a person or people, or offers to give someone a hand with their bags.

I can remember as a teacher how at recess and lunch we would "make" the children pick up papers around the campus rather than allowing the children to go play. Or worse still, we would have a "reward system" for picking up trash, which would mean that the children would only do it if they were going to get something in return. My thought was if we were going to "make" the children pick up trash as a requirement to being able to play, how sad this was, and also knowing that if we were to make them do this, that they pay a janitor *GEE* to do this, so why are we enslaving our children to do this, when they should be enjoying life! It should be done only if the children choose to out of love and caring for their immediate environment around them, not because they were "forced" or "bribed".

In contrast, to show that love and caring that I am speaking of, one night when we were driving home from a meal out, Chris insisted that we stop the car right in the middle of the parking lot by Krispy Kreme. Of course Aaron could not fathom for the life of him what on earth Chris was doing. I intuitively knew immediately what he wished to do. Without neither my husband nor I saying a word, Chris got out of the car and ran over to a spot in the parking lot that had donut papers and *Krispy Kreme* paper hats strewn from one end of this part of the parking lot, to another. He merely ran around like that of a small child being so happy to be giving a gift of love and picked up each and every wrapper and put them in the trash can a few hundred yards away. Now if that is not love of the environment, goodness in the heart and a wonderful example of manners, I do not know what is!

Chris did this from his heart, not because a teacher "forced" him to. He did it also because he has observed the many countless selfless times that my husband and I, or my father, or the older gentleman man who lives down the street from us, was kind enough to help someone without expecting anything in return. These are the things that no school can "teach" you.

Another social gift we strive to model to our children is that all people are created equal. A love of all things and all people, regardless of anything. Our children see the beauty and love in everything and everyone. And not only do they observe it, but they embrace it, and they are grateful for it too. From the sliver of that blade of grass on the lawn, to the gardener who mowed the lawn, to the lawn mower, to the all of the thousands of people it took to make that lawn mower and every trinket that goes into making that lawn mower, to the man who is homeless on the street, to the woman driving a Mercedes. We model a love of all here and an appreciation for even the tiniest of things living and nonliving free from judgment, as it does not matter if the woman driving that Mercedes has more *GEE* than we do, as we are happy for her. We do not judge her as bad or wrong for the wealth that she has. We do not judge the homeless person on the street for the fact that he is homeless or that he should as some might say "just get a job". We wish him well on his journey and offer to help if we can.

When I used to be a teacher in the public and private sector, I used to cringe at the thought of observing daily children whom were segregated and taken to a special section of the school because they were "special needs" children or because they spoke a different language. It always broke my heart. The schools could just as easily place these children with an aide which they had anyway in the "special needs room" so that these children could be a part of the group, and not feel as if they did not belong simply because they are what society deems as "different".

But because the schools are so afraid of the "liability" of what would happen to another child, they segregate the supposed "problem" child or children. And that is not to say that they should not care about the other children being hurt. What I am saying is that they should care only as a means to "cover their behinds" as it were. Even children who have what is termed as "special needs" are still children too. I believe that all can co-exist through acceptance and through accommodating all in balance. It is due to fear and lack of acceptance and accommodation that schools choose to segregate rather than join together all.

Also the children who are segregated due to the fact that they speak another language and forced to learn English, had to do so while never acknowledging the unique culture they were raised in, and not enabling the other students to learn from them. Learning, in school, comes from the books and teachers. So sad that we live in a society that values learning, let us say Spanish, from a book over learning from a Spanish speaking child within their own school. And if the school does allow it, it is not until "they" deem age appropriate.

All of this said, makes me really believe that my children are not "missing out" on the wonderful "socializations" of the schooling environment. How about you? This begs the question of what do you say to your friends and family when they ask are your children getting enough "socialization" within being a Life Long Learning family? I would say that we do not need to worry about our children being "socialized", and then explain to them why.

~

Schools have not necessarily much to do with learning ~ they are mainly institutions of control, where basic habits must be inculcated in the young. Learning is quite different and has little place in school ~ Winston Churchill

Chapter Twelve

Don't Laugh at Me ~
Life Long Learning & Labels

Labels. We use them as a means to describe the world around us. In this context, they make sense and they are a wonderful, demonstrative way to utilize language. The trouble comes in when people attempt to use labels to describe how an individual should be a certain way and how they should be treated that makes the context of labels seem rather degrading. When our boys were in the schooling environment, there was a song that they would "teach" the children there. It was a song that really resonated with me for the meaning behind the words. The school was attempting to use this song as a way to have children not be called names or made fun of by their peers. But the song for me was a way to take it one step further. Because even within this song, there are labels claiming that "well aren't we all" as a means to say that if we all are 'fat' then it is ok. The concept of the song is what resonated with me, as did some of the words, however, this type of labeling and an asking of our children to accept it in this way did not.

Our Descriptive World

If we look at words and how they are used to describe the world around us, we can see that labeling a flower as a flower gives us a means to describe that plant in nature that has petals and a stem and grows in the earth. Let us now take that same flower and add another more concise description to it and call it a fat flower. Now the label or description of that flower as a fat flower has no meaning until we place meaning upon it. And in our society, the word fat seems to have a negative context to it. Thus if that flower were actually that of a person and we were calling that individual a fat person, this would hurt this person's feelings as human beings have feelings. So given our perceptions of meaning for the word 'fat', this flower would seem to be given a perception as "bad" because we have deemed the word fat to have a negative connotation to it. Thus, this same concept also then applies to that of labeling our children. We have deemed labels such as *"ADD (Attention Deficit Disorder)"* as having a bad connotation to it.

If you look at the very label itself, it does give an essence of "negativity" to it. The word 'deficit' means that something is deficient or missing. Is there really anything missing from a child who has this supposed disorder? I rather like to view this child or children as that nothing is "missing" or "wrong" with them, that they are whole and complete just as they are. If you are to look at the word 'disorder', which means that things are in a mess or in disarray or in chaos, does that not somehow imply then that the child who has this "disorder" is a mess?

How positive, how uplifting is this label then really? Is not our objective to see our children and all children, as whole and complete just as they are? And what is the definition of normal? The truth is, there is no one definition of "normal". Normal means a variety of things to a variety of people. If you were to ask one thousand individuals what their definition of being normal in this world meant to them, you would receive 1000 completely unique answers. Why? Because each and every single one of us is unique. So should we not be celebrating these uniquenesses rather than making them appear to be "bad"? Or as if they are a mess and chaos? Society speaks of the "norm" as if there is such a large portion of the population that seems to have the exact same tendencies or that they all behave in the exact same way as others do. The truth is that because we are all unique, not a single one of us can really act the same or be the same as another. We may emulate something similar but not ever exactly the same. This is why there really is no such thing as normal.

With *ADD* then I rather prefer to change it to mean *Attention to Divine Direction*, as in that children who have a tendency to follow to the beat of their own drum and listen to the wisdom from within them, of that of their divine self, should not be punished for being the unique individuals that they are simply because they do not fit into what is considered "the norm". I believe that in society that the word "normal" seems to take on this implication of that which is distinctive than they are and that somehow this is "wrong" or "bad" for some reason because they are not the same. In other words, as an example, if you are not say, like a skilled writer, than there must be something wrong with you. Oh wait! I know, let us say then that you have "writer deficiency" and that way I look better than you, because you are not normal like me!

Fear of the Unknown

I believe that we place these labels upon children, and upon others, out of the fear of the unknown. Imagine being born with a sensory, nervous, or cranial system that perceives more than we ordinarily perceive, reacts more to stimuli than we ordinarily do, and creates in new ways than we ordinarily create. Such a child might hear sounds the rest of us do not, see colors and lights that are invisible to others, feel things in ways that we do not feel, have an inner knowledge base that is way beyond our own scope of knowledge, and physically react to food and other substances the rest of us are able to tolerate within our bodies with no trouble at all. We can say that this fear of the unknown is a Forgetting that Everything is Always, in all ways, Revolving (FEAR ~ Forgetting Everything is Always Revolving); that we are forever infinitely changing, transforming, and can be expressed within infinite possibilities.

Thus when we are to separate the infinite possibilities of what or who our children are or can be by categorizing or labeling them with 'different names', that we limit the nature of their experience and of all people's experience. Meaning, if we say that a child is "only" a child with ADD or any other disorder and that is all, this "only" then limits the infinite possibilities that they can or may be. Under the label of "only" ADD or "only" this or that, implies a separation that cuts off all other infinite possibilities of what it can BE. A label in and of itself and our children are free from any one way or from being 'right' or 'wrong', 'good' or 'bad', 'left' or 'right', 'up' or 'down' and so on infinitely; that they just simply ARE ~ A Revolving Experience of What IS, whatever that ISness IS to them of who they feel they are and of who they choose to be, rather than a "label" that we tell them they are.

Does this child then have a "syndrome" or a "disorder"? Or could it be that this child is merely advanced in another way than the rest of us in a world that has no concept of such a possibility of these new ways in existence? It is easy for us to deny the existence of anything that we have not personally experienced, that of the unknown. After all, for centuries people believed the world to be flat, and so to them the world was flat. To say anything other than that was completely inaccurate in their view, in their perception. To step outside of our belief system and attempt to view the world through the eyes of an other individual, especially through the eyes of a small child, seems to be such a difficult task for others and one of which many find to be naïve and ignorant. As their belief is that how could a child know of these things, they are just a child? We are so used to seeing the world from a "good-bad" spectrum. However, when we are able to, as a society, focus on the nonjudgmental continuum in life, we free ourselves and others to explore infinite, unlimitless possibilities.

The Good, The Bad, & The Ugly

Labels, so very much affected us as a family, which is one of many reasons why we became a Life Long Learning family. Chris, our oldest, when he was in school, was constantly told how "below standard" he was in his learning. One of his teachers was quoted on his report card as saying the following *"I cannot understand why Chris is so lazy. He does not apply himself."* This is coming from a child, whom at the age of four began tinkering with computers and by the age of six knew how to install his own software and configure a PC better than most technicians. By the time he was six, he was providing PC technical support to all of the computers within the entire school! And this is a child whom is lazy and not applying himself! It was simply that he was not applying himself to being the robot that this teacher and others wished for him to be that gave him the label of being "lazy" and "not applying himself"!

Matthew suffered yet a similar fate when in compulsory education. For the two and a half years he was there, he was told, as I was regularly told, that he could not read. I was also informed that at least four out of the five days a week; he would have to be pulled away from learning time in class to be with a reading specialist. The teachers and administrators all felt that if they did not "teach" him the "right" way that he would never learn to read. They labeled him with "dyslexia tendencies" and just as his older brother Chris when he was this same age, they wished for him to have an IEP (Individual Education Plan).

The word dyslexia literally means 'blindness'. Are our children blind? Heavens no! They just view language in another way, rather than by what is considered "normal" by societal standards. They see the world as all children see the world, through their own unique view and with their own unique beauty. Does this then make them blind? Quite the contrary. It is not that Matthew nor Chris do not know how to read or are what society calls "dyslexic". They both know how and do read beautifully. In terms of "grading" purposes and for purposes of rote memorization, no, our children do not know how to read. They know how to read for the love of reading, an enjoyment of the written word.

Our children have not learned to read by staring at a book that they may or may not like and being forced to sound out the phonetic sounds because someone told them they **had to.** Our children have learned to read when it excites them and makes a connection to their world. They read signs on the road, video games that they play, the Yu-Gi-Oh cards that they play with and more. Matthew in fact at one point, chose that he wanted to read more and more of his Yu-Gi-Oh cards so that he could learn how to play the game more efficiently. Just because they do not read within "the box" that the school places them into, does not mean that they do no know how to read. It just means that they read within how *they* choose, free from the confines of that box.

Language "Rules"

How many of our words within the English language especially, have supposed "exceptions" to the rules that were created regarding the language. How confusing is it then for a six year old to possibly know **all** these "rules" in order to read as society deems "correctly". I mean, for heaven sakes, I was an English major all through my schooling from first grade right on through college, and *I* do not even know nor remember word for word all of the "rules" of the language and how every minute detail of them are utilized! And I am a writer too! So how can we expect our children to know this?!

I remember reading an article that Sandra Dodd once wrote for *Home Education Magazine,* in which she wrote about how as a child, she remembered saying Yosemite Sam's name as YOZEmite Sam! I had to laugh at this, because my mother used to joke around with my brother and I as children all the time saying the exact same thing! Or *Yosemite National Park* the same way ~ *YOZEmite National Park*! It was a funny, but wonderful way for my mom to help us to learn how to spell and read really. It was not until I had my own children that I realized this. I so appreciate my mother for all of those little funny things like that she used to which helped me learn. There are just so many ways that we can help our children to learn how to spell, read, and write things, simply by turning those supposed "exceptions to the rule" into something fun and memorable ~ a connection for learning.

Sandra Dodd went on to say the following: *"Phonics is not a magic decoder ring. It has been said by many craftsmen that you know you are really advanced when you find the need to build your own tools. My children are really advanced readers, because each has created his or her own set of tools. They have discovered the patterns which phonics attempts to describe, and they understand them probably*

*better than anyone who has memorized them as lists of "rules,"
because they know when they work and when they do not work. In
many cases they know why a word is spelled as it is, as they are
learning the history of English as they learn to read, and they find it all
as fascinating as anything else they have learned. There is a root
word of "phonics" right in "Persephone" ~ "Persevere" people say.
Often they are grown before they discover that "persevere" is
pronounced differently by English speakers in other parts of the world.
Where learning is concerned, it is never too late and everything
counts."* It is a well known fact that most children do not even have
their fine and gross motor skills strong enough to write and read until
at least the age of ten. Thus, why we as a society force such growth
that they have a life time to learn and master is something I have
never been able to fathom. Matthew loves to write on the computer.
He does email, instant messaging, and at times spell check to able to
assist him with his learning of reading and writing. So it is never too
late to learn. Just because children do not read by the age of six, does
not mean that a child will never learn. I know people who are sixty and
are still learning to read. Learning to read is not a onetime process. It
is an evolutionary process that occurs over a lifetime.

There is a deeper effect to a child learning how to read and write on
their own, when they are ready to ~ that of confidence. Confidence in
the knowledge that they know how to read and write because they not
only learned of their own volition, but because they chose of their own
volition to read and write, not because someone made them learn to
read and write. Now, I do not fault the teachers at all whom attempted
to place our two children into the "boxes" that they did. Speaking as a
former teacher, whom taught from preschool all the way to second
grade, I know on a personal level, all that a teacher must endure
within this chosen career. I do say chosen, as teachers do not choose
to be teachers for any other reason than simply to help our future
generations to flourish. However, it is the way in which society has
placed teachers within a box that teachers operate in the only way
that they can. One person, whom has anywhere from twelve to as
many as thirty-five children to care for, cannot possibly give to the
child or children who are in need one on one assistance with learning
that help. And especially not of what, when, where, and how a child
wishes to learn. Can you just imagine what having thirty-five children
all wishing to learn thirty-five different things? The teacher would end
up in the insanity ward of a hospital!

Thus, within the confines of what society has allotted within this
institutionalized learning modality, this is all teachers know how to do.
Our society, as a whole, just simply sits by and allows this to go on,

without opening its eyes to see that there is another way. To look at the cost, the price that our children have to pay for this lack of knowledge and acceptance of other modalities of learning. Which is where Life Long Learning comes in ~ providing the infinite possibilities that life has to offer ~ in a way of learning that does not institutionalize learning. It is up to us as a societal whole to transform this for the future generations to come.

Son-Rise Program

A program that does just this, that has helped thousands of children and families all over the globe view *Autism* in just this manner is *The Son-Rise Program®. The Son-Rise Program®* utilizes unconditional acceptance to create a means of others joining a child's world, rather than the world forced upon the child. As quoted from their website, *http://www.son-rise.org* below, is what the program's aim is:

- **Joining in a child's repetitive and ritualistic behaviors** supplies the key to unlocking the mystery of these behaviors and facilitates eye contact, social development and the inclusion of others in play.
- **Utilizing a child's own motivation** advances learning and builds the foundation for education and skill acquisition.
- **Learning through interactive play** results in effective and meaningful socialization and communication.
- **Using energy, excitement and enthusiasm** engages the child and inspires a continuous love of learning and interaction.
- **Employing a nonjudgmental and optimistic attitude** maximizes the child's enjoyment, attention and desire throughout their *Son-Rise Program*.
- **Placing the parent** as the child's most important and lasting resource provides a consistent and compelling focus for training, education, and inspiration.
- **Creating a safe, distraction free work/play area** facilitates the optimal environment for learning and growth.

I believe that the *Son-Rise Program®* is a wonderful example of principles that we should all be incorporating with our children, whether or not they have special needs or not. I believe the level of respect of and given to the children that is shown through this program, which may very well be unique, as we are not a culture that consistently respects its children, is something that should be considered as the new "norm" if you will. In order for this to be the norm, it will require a total transformation of beliefs on the part of all. We must come to view and belief without hesitation, without doubt, and free from judgment that a child is totally loveable and acceptable just the way they are. Just as we viewed our children when we first held them in our arms as babies. When this paradigm shift occurs, it is amazing what miraculous things can occur. Because within this shift, an amazing concept begins to come to life ~ What you believe creates your reality! Yes, this may be a hard concept for some to wrap their consciousness around, but it is so very true to form, so very true to life.

Self-fulfilling Prophecies

Have you ever heard of the "Pygmalion Effect"? In 1968, there was a Harvard Study performed by Harvard researchers Rosenthal and Jacobson. Children were picked at random and their instructors were told that these children were intellectually off of the charts that could be expected to exceed their expectations during the year. True to form…by the end of the year, those children had exceeded the expectation, simply because their instructors held the expectation that they would do so. Let's take this one step further now. It is a known fact that we are all one, we are all connected. Thus, what beliefs are held by others around you also helps to create your reality. What we believe about someone often comes true, merely because our beliefs can have such a powerful effect on those around us.

An example of this comes from the musical *"My Fair Lady"*. In George Bernard Shaw's classic tale of Pygmalion, known as *"My Fair Lady"*, a sophisticated professor of phonetics bets his friend that he can take a common flower girl and transform her into a woman. Being that the theory behind the Pygmalion effect is that a person will act the way you treat them, that one's own beliefs and expectations, and that of the belief's and expectations of others, create self-fulfilling prophecies is the premise behind the story line of this musical. Thus, as Professor Higgins treats Ms. Doolittle like a woman, she starts to believe that she is a woman and behave as a woman. Unfortunately, where labeling others and what those labels represent comes in is when we often come to expect less of a child that has been labeled with a "disorder" or "syndrome" due to the connotation of that label. We expect that they will act or be a certain way, and therefore, we get exactly what it is that we expect. This is where I believe, schools and society as a whole, fail our children terribly. If we expect to have children respect us, then we must learn also to respect them. It is a two-way highway in this.

We Are the Elders

We are the Elders. No, I do not mean that we are old! We are the wise ones, all of us. Our children, they are the Elders in that they bring to us the new wisdom of viewing life from a new perspective that we may not have ever considered before. This is the way in which they are the wise ones. They have so much that they wish to share with us, this new wisdom, and we have so much to learn from them. We, the adults, are the Elders too in another distinct way. We are the voice of experience that can lead the way for our Elder children. When the new wisdom comes forth from them, we are the co-pilots to show them how to steer their course on the road of life. We show them not only the path that is uniquely their own, but also how to navigate their way through a world bent on hostility, intolerance, and judgment.

We are the ones who are to be there to stand with them in front of the mirror that shows them who they are. To ask them what it is that they see, so that we may see the world through their eyes. We are the Elders that need steadily to encourage them to find and walk their own path and to create their own realities, and not that of others. When the shadows appear in their mirrors, we urge them to confront them and to help them to know that the power that is within them is greater than that of all outside influences and oppositions. And in turn, doing this will then come full circle back to us. As then our children, who are also the Elders, reflect back to us this same way of life that we give to them, of which they then guide us and we learn from them, as we continue to guide them and they learn from us ~ thus there is a never-ending circle of learning, of love, and of life.

We need to understand that everything we share with our children and our children with us is out of mutual respect. That we can play and learn with and from our children regardless of our age or theirs ~ not having to take life so seriously, but to remain in touch with the child within us and seeing the world from our children's view. That we can learn from and with our child, free from labels and judgments. We, and those other Elders around our children, need to create the reality of unconditional love and acceptance, free from judgmental labels and wholly love and accept all ~ perfect, whole and complete, just as we are. If we are to utilize labels at all, it should be done so in a loving manner and to provide a basis of describing that of what is, not in the manner they are utilized by society now as in how a child should or should not be.

The ancient ways of learning allowed for a person, adult and child alike, to choose who their Master, their Guide would be. Later, these very Masters began choosing whom their apprentices should be, and what "criteria" they should meet in order to be one. Out of this came what we now call modern education, or the "institutional learning" today known as school. The ancient Elders believed that it takes a village to raise a child, with the implication being that there is no one way to learn and no one person to learn from. I believe the ancient Elders were correct. Now it is up to us, to show the way, as the tide is changing once again, to a new principle of returning to the ancient ways. As Joey Klien once wrote, *"As I have worked with other people around the country, helping them to heal, they begin to change, and later begin to cause change. As we continue to cherish one another, granting one another acceptance and forgiveness, one by one, we begin to shift consciousness around us. We begin to heal the world. Others may not see what I see right now, but they will. When we heal one, we heal all."* No truer words were ever written!

Some people have asked me, "Why have you chosen the word 'unlimitless', does that not imply a rigidness and a lack of limits?" Quite the contrary actually; I have purposefully made it editorially this way, as well as what editors and others might call "grammatical faux pas" within this book. One of my inspirations for doing so came from *The Mother Tongue* by Bill Bryson ISBN: 0380715430. As you will see within reading this book, the language that we have here on this earth is simply free from being as it appears to be. Thus, this word 'unlimitless' is a play on words, just like that of the play on words we utilize when "labeling" children with things such as ADD, autism, etc. This play on words can be so damaging to a child's self worth and love of learning when utilized in this context. This word 'unlimitless' is to remind us of this and to know that the word unlimitless means that there really is no limit to the learning available within Life Long Learning. The reasoning for this word then is to show how labeling when perceived in a fashion of "wrong" or somehow "bad" that we really are limiting our ways of seeing beyond that label to view the child for who they are ~ whole, complete, and full of unlimitless potential for and of learning.

~

Learning is not the filling of a pail, but the lighting of a fire ~ William Butler Yeats

Chapter Thirteen

Life Long Learning Buffet

Do you remember when our children were first born? Do you remember that they ate when they were hungry? Do you remember that we would nurse them or bottle feed them when they needed nourishment?

With our boys, each one of them set their own feeding patterns. Each one of them ate when they were hungry. They instinctively knew when they were hungry and they would eat at the given time they were hungry. At about the age of four or five months though somehow this all changes. We begin to impart the concept of a "schedule" upon our children. We basically tell them when to eat, how much to eat, and what to eat.

Growing up as a child, my mother would feed us three square meals a day with one snack right after school, and she made us the food and we were made to eat what was given to us. Not that my mother's intentions were "bad", as they were neither "good nor bad", "right nor wrong". She only did what she knew how to do, what was handed down to her and for that I am grateful to her for being the wonderful mom she is, as I love her very much.

The thing of it is, however well intentioned we feel we are as parents, forcing our children to eat what we feel is best for them, may quite possibly turn out quite the opposite. The reason I say this goes back to chapter three in that of choice. When we "schedule" our children's meals for them, choosing for them what they will and will not eat, when and how, we are not allowing for choice.

Why?

Let's look at this from another perspective. As an adult, if someone were to cook you something to eat when you were not hungry and tell you that you must sit down and eat it all because it is "good for you" and you were not going to get up from the table until you ate it all, how would this resonate with you? This would seem like a rather harsh and cruel thing to do. Yet, this is exactly what we do to our children when enforcing the "schedule" of eating.

Children are no different than adults in terms of their innate ability to know when they are hungry and what their body needs in terms of nutrition. I believe that one of the contributing factors to the weight issues in society today is very simply because we have been "trained" by the clock that says that it is lunch time and therefore we should eat, regardless of whether we are hungry or not. Another contributing factor is that since most of us feel that we should eat those three meals a day, simply because someone said we should, that at dinner time, we often feel guilty for knowing that we will somehow be "bad" if we do not eat **now,** because we have been told that it is simply "unwise" to eat after a certain hour, and so therefore we gorge ourselves in order to feel full enough to last until morning. It is therefore, that I believe that the weight issues in this world are attributed more to how much we eat, why we eat, and what we eat, rather than simply lack of exercise and just "watching" what we eat.

So, why is it then that a child is born with the innate ability to know when to eat and yet, we squash this well before the time they are a year old? We squash a child's intuitive ability to listen to their own bodies to know when they are hungry and also when they are full as they once did as small babies. Thus by the time children reach the age of four or five, they have lost the ability of their own internal power to stop eating, as they do not know when they are full. They only know to stop eating when their plate is empty as a way of knowing when they are full, regardless if their body really needs all of the food or not and so they keep eating and eating. They also lose the ability to know when they are hungry and begin to eat food simply because it is put I front of them because it is "dinner time" or because we say "Oh look! It is 2 p.m. *way* past your lunch time, you must be starving!" In losing the ability to listen to our own body's internal messages for food, the way we first did as a baby, we then spend the rest of our lives and our children do as well, struggling to regulate food intake simply because we were never given the choice to learn on our own as children.

Why is it we do this to our children? Why was this done to ourselves as children? And our parents as children? and so on...Why? Because someone said so! Someone said at some point in our history that eating three meals a day is what we all must do. Because someone said that eating carrots is part of the "healthy diet". And what of the word diet. Have you ever noticed that within the word 'diet' is the word die? This is because a bit of our spirit dies each time we are not allowed to listen to our own body's internal messages for what it needs in terms of food. This is why "diets" do not work, because we are denying what our body is attempting to tell us. Our spirit is *dying* inside, when we go with what someone else tells us is right for our bodies, rather than listening to what our body tells us.

All of the studies and research has been done in an attempt to prove what is "the right thing to do" when it comes to eating, when the truth is, the only person who truly knows what is right for your body and when and how it is right for it, is **YOU!** Even children as young as four or five months old, while they cannot talk, can still let you know in other ways what it is they like and do not like when we try a variety of foods with them.

We spend so much time trusting and believing in what other people and so-called "experts' say about our eating, that we do not rely upon ourselves to know what is best. We act as if we are robots needing to be programmed to tell us when to eat, what to eat, and how much to eat, as if we cannot think and feel within our own bodies how to do this. And why? Because we were told as a baby that our own internal body was not correct, that our parents and all of the "experts" know best, better than we do! If we cannot trust our own selves to know what is best for us, then why are we so trusting of others to lead us? Should we not be leading ourselves by listening to our own intuitive bodies messages?

Deschooling Food

I have to say that deschooling food in our house has been one of the most fun and exciting aspects of Life Long Learning. Our children knowing that they have the freedom to eat what they want, when they want, and how they want has been such a freeing adventure. We have always let our children know from the very beginning, that if they cannot finish whatever it is that is on their plate, that it is ok, that it always can be saved and put away until later. Or if at a restaurant, we can take it home to be eaten later. I know of some parents who get very upset at the fact that when eating at a restaurant that their children will order something, only to eat very little or none of it and claim they are hungry in the car on the way home or later.

My thought is, if this happens, it should be no big deal. So you take the food home, and you or someone else in the family if not your child, eats it later. If they are hungry in the car, offer to make them something else when you get home if they do not wish to eat what was left over from their food at the restaurant. Did the food go to waste? No, I do not believe it was as it can be utilized at another time is all. Was the *GEE* wasted on that food? Again, I would say no, because it will still be eaten, whether it was your child who ended up eating it, or if it was you or someone else, it will be eaten, therefore the *GEE* was not wasted on purchasing the food.

In our family, we eat when we are hungry ~ whether this be at what is deemed by society as 'Lunch' or 'Dinner', or if it is by the standards of the societal clock at 2 a.m. We try to have at least one meal a day where we all eat together. There have been many times though that one or more of us in the house are not hungry, and if this is the case, we still all sit and enjoy each other's company, while not feeling obligated to eat simply because someone else is. The focus then becomes not on the food as much as the opportunity for connection and togetherness as a family, a way to bond with each other.

What we eat and how much we eat has transformed over the years as well. While I admit, there are some things we eat that are considered "unhealthy" by certain standards; we do eat a wide variety of foods. We have found that we eat less simply because there is not this need to hoard food for fear of not being able to eat again until a certain "time". We listen to our own individual body messages and we eat until we are full. We know now when we are full or when we are hungry, because in deschooling food we have allowed our own bodies natural rhythms to kick back in on their own and we listen to them.

We also find that as a family we all react differently to certain foods and certain types of foods. By listening to our bodies natural rhythms, we adjust our grocery list accordingly, not because someone told us to, but because our own individual bodies told us to.

Allergies

For instance, Anthony has discovered, not through anything that anyone has said to him or done, but he has discovered through listening to is own body that things that have too much sugar in them within a matter of a few moments can give him a stomach ache. He starts to get headaches and generally not feel well in addition to the stomach aches. Therefore, not because it is "bad" for him or because mommy or daddy said so, but because he experienced it for himself, Anthony chooses now not to eat sugar for the most part. He also knows that in those times that he does, that this is what will occur for him.

For Chris, he has discovered that eating too many fried and processed foods makes his skin break out. For Matthew, he has discovered that since we now eat less at any one given time we do eat, when he does fall back into the eating to hoard because of that "I am afraid that I will not be able to later" stage, his body reacts in a rather unpleasant way. He will develop stomach aches and diarrhea from an overload of food in his system, as his body is not used to doing that anymore. For my husband Aaron, he has found that an overgrowth of yeast in his body and allergy to sugar causes his athlete's foot, leg infections, and an overall ill feeling within his body. And for me, with the two life threatening illnesses that I have been told by conventional medicine that I have, for me, too much protein in the way of meat I have found cause gallbladder attacks. Too many greasy or acidic foods do as well.

The only way we were able to discover this was by listening to our bodies and adjusting accordingly. When in the schooling environment and/or living a life that is so hectic and busy, we often do not take the time to slow ourselves down enough to listen truly to what our bodies need. We simply rely on others to give us the information about our bodies and what it reacts to and does not react to, when it is only our body that truly knows. This is why all diets and life style changes relating to eating do not work the same for each person. As we are all unique, and each of our bodies is unique. So what one diet or way of eating works for one person, may or may not work for another.

An example of this happened in my own life a few years ago. A good friend of mine at the time was doing the famous Atkins diet. She wanted me to join her in doing so. Intuitively I knew that my body would not respond favorably to it. A few days later, I found out why. The Atkins diet is based upon lowering carbs and raising protein. The raising of proteins comes from eating meat constantly primarily as well as eggs, chicken, and other forms of protein. For me raising my protein levels too high in this fashion is like a death sentence, because too high of protein causes me gallbladder and liver attacks and could cause my liver to fail, ergo I would literally die or this diet! Upon doing my research and discovering this, I respectfully declined my friends' invitation to join her.

Shopping

As a Life Long Learning family, trips to the store become a learning adventure. I used to make a list of what we were "supposed" to get.

Now it is more of a list of reference as to not forget certain things such as butter or tortillas or items that we may specifically need for a meal that we are planning to eat together that day.

When we shop together, our children choose what they want to eat within our *GEE* budget for groceries of course. They know that say we have only 150 *GEE's* to spend today while we are in the store. We either plan before hand or just explore the store for the items that strike us in that moment that we wish to eat for the week. We all are human, and we all have likes and dislikes, and this allows them the freedom to see all choice within the store, have the knowledge of what is considered by certain standards to be "good" or "bad" for you food and of what does or does not affect their bodies in certain ways, and they choose what it is they wish to eat for the week.

If our children choose something that affects their body in a certain way, I may gently remind them of that and ask if they considered this before they place it in the basket. If they have, and they still choose that particular item, then they still choose it and are aware of the consequences for that choice whatever those consequences are.

I must say because our children have been given this freedom of choice that they do choose what my husband and I consider to be wise choices when it comes to food and shopping. But more importantly, they have come to choose foods that are deemed by standards as healthy, because they wish to eat it, not because mom and dad say so.

I think it is really important that we in this society begin to treat food for what is ~ Food. I believe we should stop treating certain foods as junk or bad. Food is just food. It is whatever perception we place upon it is the label it becomes. When we continue to attach labels to the food our children eat, or that we eat, children pick up on that. In picking up on that, it gives our children the tendency to feel bad about themselves for eating the "wrong" food. Food, nor our children, are bad, good, or right or wrong, they just are who and what they are. Let food just be what it is ~ Food.

Short Order Cook

When we remove the "have to's" and the "should's" given to us by others, we are then able to free our minds from the robotic imprisonment it has been in for all these years in our relationship to food. It allows our children to be free to make choices with food as we do as adults. It also allows our bodies to fall back into that state of being in tuned with our minds again so that we are able to choose for ourselves when we choose to eat, how we choose to eat, and how much we choose to eat based upon our body, not based upon a pre-determined schedule or guideline given to us by others whom do not understand our bodies.

When it comes to eating, whether we are at home eating, or going out, everyone in our family, child, and adult alike, chooses what they wish to eat, when it comes to meals. Usually, if we are eating at home, we will occasionally plan a meal for all of us to eat. However, if one or more of us chooses not to eat what is made, whomever is making the meal that night, or whomever is asking to make something else for that person does.

Some people will ask me, well does that not make you feel as if you are a short order cook? The answer I give them is 'No', and here is why. Whether our children are old enough to cook or not, whether my husband is able to or not, I prefer to see my meal preparation as a gift of love. A gift of love that I give freely to my family because I love them.

I never feel like I do not have the time to cook for my family. I feel that coming forth in the manner of not "having enough time" seems to say that I do not have enough time for, do not appreciate, and love my family. I believe that one should always have time for the ones that they love, and if they do not, that they should make the time. As when you are going with the flow of life, rather than against it, life flows right along with you. The things that you felt that you did not have time for, you find that you suddenly do. It is only when we fight the flow of life, that give us our feelings of "I do not have enough time" or those feeling of "I am a short order cook".

Also, is the consideration that in life, people do not make us feel something, such as when we say statements like this, "he is making feel like a short order cook". No one can "make us" do anything that we do not choose to. We are all give free will, and that free will includes that of choice. Therefore it is each of us who choose how we feel, rather than someone "doing" something to us or "making" us feel something. We choose our reactions to people in life, as we cannot control or change others, we can only simply control or change our reactions to others.

Therefore, I do not consider it to be a hassle nor do I consider them being "too picky" for wanting to eat what it is that they want to eat. I consider it an honor that our children have chosen and requested of me to give them the gift of cooking something special for them. When a gift is given from a space of love and caring for another than it should never be considered a bother or a chore. It should be done out of love and a true genuineness to see the other person happy. Whether it be cooking a meal for someone, or picking up after them or doing their laundry. Being in service to others without judgment, without anger, but in total and complete love is one of the main reasons why we are here in this lifetime. It is what is called living your life "on purpose".

How many times do we do kind things for others? ~ friends or maybe even a person of whom we never met ~ yet, the people we seem to love most, we have such a hard time wrapping our consciousness around helping. What if we were to change, transform our perception just a bit? Enough to see that cooking separate meals for each person in your family as a way of giving a loving bundle of food gift. The same as we give a gift meal basket to a friend when they are ill and cannot cook for themselves or as we feel when we are giving that same gift of food in feeding a homeless person who has no food.

If we are able to view cooking for our family, no matter what form it takes, whether it be all separate meals or just one, as a gift of love that we give freely ~ free from boundaries or conditions, but just coming from a space of the love we have for them, it gives life so much more of a flow to it.

Feeling Meals

Have you ever noticed too, how if you are preparing meal for someone and you are angry or are upset or feel as if you do not "have the time" to cook for your family, that the person eating that meal ends up not feeling good later on or has a bad reaction to the food? Now aside from the obvious fact that it could be food poisoning or that they just did not feel well, this can also be because whomever the preparer of that meal is, whether it be the chef at a local restaurant, or you yourself, since we are all made up of energy, that anger, those upset feelings, they transfer as energy into our food. Then when we ingest that food, we ingest the upset and angry energy right along with it, thereby, making us feel ill later on. Try this as an experiment sometime. Observe what happens to you or others around you when you have digested someone else's anger and upset feelings within a cooked meal.

Cooking separate meals can also at times give a basis, a way for you to enjoy cooking together should you and your child(ren) so choose. I know many a times when I will be making that extra meal for one of our boys, they will come up to me and ask if the can help make the meal that they wish to have. This provides us with bonding time, learning time, and just plain old fashioned fun! We sing while we cook, we laugh, we talk, we learn, we just enjoy being together and being in the moment. And when a meal is made with love, and during those times where the meal is prepare of our child or children's own hands, man it just tastes *so* wonderful!

At times during the day, when our boys get hungry and we are not making a sit down type of meal, they simply go into the kitchen and fix themselves something to eat. We have as parents, never placed a limit on whether they were "too young" or not "old enough" to cook something for themselves. Being that Matthew is 8 and Anthony 7 at the time that this book is to be published, should they require help with the stove or some other gadget in the kitchen, I am or Aaron is always right there to assist if need be. My feeling is if they wish to learn how to cook something, then they are "old enough" to learn. And when they do cook their own meals, in whole or in part, it gives our children a great sense of satisfaction from fixing their own foods that they eat ~ that competence and capability.

Thus meal time in our home, never "makes me feel" like a short order cook. Now, I have to say, though, that we do jokingly pretend to ring a bell, not due to feeling like a short order cook, but because of the counter that is within the kitchen in the home we currently live in. It was built higher for stools to be place underneath, so that when you sit at it to eat there it reminds me of one of those restaurant bar counters where they go *Ding!* with the bell and they say, "Your order is up!" Thus, now the joke is that Chris will go over to the rice steamer and turn the knob on it back and forth so that it dings the bell, and of course we all laugh!

We usually try to keep on hand in the house, all of the items that our boys enjoy that they can make for themselves, so that if they wish to make something, it is accessible to them. More often then not, they love it when I, when mom cooks. There is just something about a mom's cooking that brings out the love and caring in all of us. It is like that feeling of coming home again, like when you were a baby. If that is who I am for my boys, that feeling of unconditional love and of home then who I am to take that from them by selfishly calling myself a "short order cook".

~

We worry about what a child will be tomorrow, yet we forget that he is someone today ~ Stacia Tauscher

I am learning all the time, the tombstone will be my diploma ~ Eartha Kitt

Chapter Fourteen

The College Creation

Ah! So now you have either reached the point where your child has now blossomed into that of a teenager, and you are considering the notion that your child may want to pursue college. Or you have now come to the place where you understand fully and can embrace the idea of being a Life Long Learning family until that big 'C' word. Or better still, you are just like the majority of us who are just reading this book chapter by chapter and have found yourself at this chapter!

Either way, Welcome! You have made it! No matter where you are at, there you are. You made it to this point in your journey, and in the journey of this book.

So, what of that 'C' word ~ College???

Well, I could still here in this chapter and write all about the advantages of college, and about how if you begin around as early of an age as say 10 or 11, that you can have your child in a community college, taking whatever courses are available for them to take at that point in their lives and whatever they are interested in pursuing, and how wonderful it will be to have a jump start on that college education! Because after all, it is so ever important to have that degree to show you can **become** something in this world, in this society, and how without it, you will spend your life just working to get by, right?

I could say all this and much, much more, and provide all of the tips to get into the right colleges for each career. I could show you how to write up the transcripts from your private school you set up every year so that "legally" you can be a Life Long Learning family according to whatever laws or bylaws your state or country dictate and all.....

I could write all about all of this.......but I am not going to. I am not going to because it has all been written about before. There are a gazillion books and internet and CD Rom resources out there about how to write up transcripts and how to get into the right colleges after homelearning for all or part of your children's lives. If you choose to, you can go search out and find this information, as this type of information will not be what you will find in this chapter.

And if you believe that a college degree is the only way to make it in this world, then nothing I write here in this book, will change your mind. In the almost two hundred pages that this book has transformed into being, my aim was never nor is ever to change your mind. As I cannot change your mind, or you. I have no power to do that. The only person whom can change your perception about something is you! Yes, that is right, only you can do this. No one can *make* you change your perception, not I, not the leaders of your country, not even the world's most profound leader can do this, but *you*!

Why do you ask? Because you have what is known as free will. Yes, as we talked about in chapter three, you have free will. You have free will to choose, always, even when you feel you do not even have a choice, you still have a choice. If you do not remember about this, I would respectfully request that you go back and re-read chapter three.

Rather than give you tips and wisdom of college in the conventional ways, I invite you to take a moment to view college from another point of view. Yes, just view it. You do not have to adopt it or embrace it, if you do not choose to. I invite you to check it out, try on the concept, and then just like that of the rest of this book, if it fits you and you wish to choose to transform your perception, your way of thinking in this area, and adopt this concept, this philosophy, well then congratulations to you. However, if you feel that this is not a fit for you, just like that of this book, then do nothing with the wisdom that I offer to you within this chapter, or within the pages of this book and that is ok as well.

The choice is up to you. Whichever you choose, is a choice that is not right or wrong, not good nor bad, just that of what you choose. I do not judge you one way or another for that choice, as this is not who I am. All I ask within this book is that you look outside, around, through, in-between the box ~ view it and take it into your being, and then when all of the information and wisdom is absorbed within you, that you see for yourself, what parts of this chapter, of this book work for you and which do not. And if that is all of it, then that is great, and if it is none of it, then this is great as well. But just to know that your choice is based up viewing the outside of the box, the inside of the box, and from all angles of possibility and then making a choice is the only wish that I have for you.

Outside of the 'C' Word Box and into the New 'C' Word!

We are beings of creation. We came from that of which was created by the love and the ectoplasm of our parents. As human beings we are constantly in a state of creating. Creation gives birth, gives life to possibility. And as such that we are all beings of creation, we can create anything we desire.

As such, we are always creating. Homelearning laws enable us in most states and countries, to be able to be Life Long Learners legally without interference from that state or country. Although depending upon those laws, which do vary from state to state, country to country, we are able to through these laws from the ages of birth through legal adult age (which in most places is the age of 18), are able to have this space of freedom.

But, what about College? I believe that since we are such amazing creating human beings, that we can therefore create a wonderful approach to carry the Life Long Learning beyond ~ that of creating our own College.

Say what? What did I just write you ask? Create my own what? Yes, that is correct, you were not just seeing things; I did say create your own college. Find what it is that interests you that you wish to learn and create your own college.

There is a young woman by the name of Heather Martin who did just that several years ago. Her website is located at:

http://www.homestead.com/peaceandcarrots/CollegeHowTo.html and

http://www.homestead.com/peaceandcarrots/Orion.html

Heather is a Life Long Learner, who upon "graduating" legally from her studies at the age of 18, chose to continue the learning, and thus created her own college O.R.I.O.N. Her college studies include Outdoor Recreation, Environmental Education, Alternative Medicine, and Photography. She has listed all of her courses and assignments that she completed as a part of her college experience. On her websites, Heather also gives tips on how to create transcripts, how to create your College Degree, and what to do to make your portfolio look professional and ready to be utilized on job interviews with potential employers in your given field.

It also gives you a wonderful way also to take the college you create and the degree you receive from your college, and go into business for yourself. There are many ways one can go into business for themselves. Part of the college courses actually can be in Business

Management if one so chooses, to learn how to run a business in your chosen field.

Anyone can create their own College. Conventional colleges, nor trade schools, are not the end all be all necessity to getting that job or opening the business you wish to have in your chosen career. Anyone over the age of 18 can create their own college, making it like a business. You would have to look into your local and state laws concerning a business license and what the process is and the cost involved. I know here in the area of California we live in, it costs only 17 *GEE's* ($17) for a business license. You might also wish to spend the money to obtain a separate phone line either cell phone or that of a land line to have a phone number with a voice mail attached for potential employers to contact if they are looking for verification of your degree and course of study.

There are many businesses that do this today, offering courses with degrees, and diplomas, that are not accredited and some are. Some have made their own accreditation as another business, thereby accreditating their own college that way. Who is to say that you cannot do so? As long as it is within your local laws, the sky is the limit! We pay many of these colleges online or in person to attend their college, why not create our own, and do the same thing!

In fact, I have done just this. I studied to become an Aromatherapist, as well as many other courses and as such, I paid for courses through a small but growing accredited college of whom awarded me this certification. Had I thought of or known of Heather's concept at the time, I could have saved my self many *GEE's* on this venture.

Heather makes a point of stating on her website that there are a lot of credible unaccredited colleges operating in every state or country. Yale, Harvard, and Princeton were all unaccredited at one time. It does not make your studying and your degree worth less if your college is not accredited. What matters is the level of learning and being able to in the society in which we live in, to present what is considered by society to be a valid way of showing that learning out in the world in your chosen profession.

She also makes a point of stating that when you feel you are ready to "graduate" and obtain your degree, that you do so. Now, some of you may ask me, "Does this not degrade and humiliate all of those people who spend the *GEE's* and work **so** hard to obtain their college degree the "right" way?" Well, first, I will say this, who is it that determined it to be the "right" way in the first place? Just because someone said so many years ago! As I spoke of earlier in this book, there is no right way or wrong way to life your life, or for your child to life their life. Our child or children, just as we do, live our lives as we live our lives. It is just what is.

Who is also to say that the person who creates their own college and obtains a degree does not work just as hard if not harder in some cases, than that of the person whom attends a four year university? I actually believe that the person who creates the college of their own volition is in some cases learning more and works harder. Because the person who goes to a four year university, having the passion for their chosen career, simply go forth and learn about that chosen career. They will go from one class to another and listen to lectures, and do the assignments and "make the grade" in order to receive that degree. Half or better of the time they spend is on repeating basic courses such as Math and English as a part of that, while not spending as much time on their field of study (with the exception of achieving a Master's in college, where you the devote more time on your chosen career).

While this involves much reading, work, studying, and in some cases some hands-on learning, the individual who creates their own college must do the legwork that involves the creation of their chosen field of study. From the creation of the college as a business, running of that business, creation of courses of study, transcripts, assignments, materials to be used, methods of learning, how these methods of learning will come to fruition, and the creation of the degrees themselves. Then they also have to have that passion for that chosen career and go forth and learn about that chosen career. Most of the focus of a individual who has created their own college then is precisely on their chosen career, and not on repetitive courses that have already been learned such as Math and English, unless it is apart of the learning for their degree, such as that of a career as an English or Math instructor.

Neither way for college is right or wrong. All ways, be it going to a university, community college, a trade school, or that of creating your own college, are all valid ways to approach learning within the college modality. It is up to you to choose which one works best for you. This is just a means of showing that there is another way, if you look outside the box of what society tells us that must be, to see that there is another way, there are unlimitless possibilities that are available in Life Long Learning. Thus, I do not believe that the creation of one's own college is degrading or humiliating anyone or anything. It is just an ingenious way to expand and enhance a way of learning in life, an addition to the long list of options that are available to you, to our children, through ours and their lives.

While I would agree that college does have it's place here in this world, as the world is right now ~ as many Doctors, Lawyers, Scientists, and Engineers etc. were and are required to have this book and in some cases hands-on learning through a degree provided by a college, because this I just how society as a general whole works at this time on this earth. Within these given professions, college is seen then by society as quite important and quite necessary. It was not always this way. As before there were colleges, there was knowledge and wisdom, and that knowledge and wisdom were the only "requirements" to know what you knew and to be able to live and work doing what you love.

I believe that in the not so-distant future that we will see ourselves living by our own learning clocks. I believe that we will see a change, a transformation if you will, within the methods of learning modalities that society has. To where society as a whole will begin to see and recognize individuals as revered for their life experience, knowledge, and wisdom within a certain career of their choosing, and be allotted jobs based upon solely that, rather that upon a simple piece of paper that tells others that this person must "know" their given profession based solely on the piece of paper. In the not so-distant future, we will come to know, understand, embrace, and utilize the expertise of people based upon their sharing and demonstrating their wisdom and not because of a piece of paper that says so.

So do I worry if our children will be going to college? Heavens no. Why? Because whatever learning modality they choose ~ whether it be college, trade school, that of their own college, or any other modality that they choose to learn, the learning is just going to keep on continuing for the rest of their lives. We do not stop learning simply because we "graduated" a college and earn a "degree" or become the age of 18.

Nor do we stop knowing all there is to know about any given career simply because we receive a "degree" either. In actuality, many given careers nowadays have what is known as "continuing education" or "continued learning" within that career. It also is often paid for by the company you work for in any given field. Company's today, know and understand this concept of that you do not stop learning once you simply get that "degree", that continued learning of new things within the field, while reviewing the basics of the given field from time to time, helps not only the individual to grow, but also that of the company's business to grow. For if we are not learning, we stagnate in life, and we die.

It is society is who is demanding that we show a piece of paper of accumulated "knowledge", in order for society to be accepting of what it is we know, of our wisdom and expertise. The thing is, we do not really need that piece of paper to know what we know, to learn what we learn, to apply and utilize what we learn. We simply need to utilize what we learn and continue to learn is how we come to know what we know and utilize what we know. We simply learn. We learn all our life long. Life Long Learning.

~

While raising my children, I lost my mind
but found my soul ~ Unknown

Learning is what remains after one has forgotten
everything he learned in school ~ Einstein

Chapter Fifteen

The Ultimate Question ~
How do I Know if My Child is Progressing?

So it is that we come to the ultimate question ~ which why I saved this chapter for last. How do I know if my child is progressing?

Life Long Learning ~ We have spent the last fourteen chapters discussing and re-discussing how wonderful, awe-inspiring, and amazing learning can be. We have seen how we can utilize these all of Life Long Learning concepts to bedtime rituals, to eating, to video gaming, to television viewing, to chores ~ to everything and to anything in life. Life Long Learning encompasses all.

We have come to know that our children will learn because it's what they were born to do, it is what their bodies, and minds have been created by us of our miraculous wonder, to do ~ learn. Learning is how the human species survives, thrives, evolves, and flourishes.

Just like when they were that little bundle of joy that you always used to love sitting on the floor with and playing puzzles and rolling the ball with them. It is a continuation of that learning that you began so many years ago, when learning was free and easy, and not full of such demands of memorization and tests. When you were free to just be, to just learn as only you and your child wish to learn ~ when, how, what, and where you wish to learn.

How do we know that our child is progressing and learning through life? It is impossible to measure the success of Life Long Learning with tests, grades, and scores. Jumping through academic hoops will not necessarily lead to self discovery. Our children gain a sense of how important self discovery is by watching us. Our ability to model self discovery in life is much more powerful than handing in book reports on time.

Helping children reach their own goals will mean there will be plenty of opportunities to discuss perseverance, follow through, and how sometimes it is worth doing the things that are no fun in order to reach the desired goal. These lessons have much more meaning when they are in conjunction with goals the children set for themselves.

Perhaps the most interesting successes are found among those children who do not flourish in a traditional setting with those standard measurements of success. The best way to know that your child is learning and progressing is ~ by listening to them speak, by watching them play, and just by **being** with them. You will know they are learning at 10, the same way you knew that they were learning at 10 months. You will see them use their skills, their knowledge, and their wisdom.

This does take some effort on the part of you as their parent. You are your child's facilitator and cheerleader. The one whom embraces life and learning with curiosity and enthusiasm with your children. You will not find your child's learning contained in the pages of a workbook or within a book report. It is not all prepared "neat and tidy" with a grade. It is spread out over the course of the day, over the course of theirs and yours lives, while you are living your lives. You have to be observant and tuned into your child, in order to know.

One of the most blessed things about Life Long Learning is that it is awe inspiring to observe the wonderment in your child moment by moment. Because, in life, all we have is just this moment....until the next moment comes along. Just to be in that moment with your child, is one of life's greatest gifts. To be so in tune with them and their lives and to have them be so in tuned with yours. It brings about a true sense of freedom, serenity, and contentment...... and is that not how life should be?

Learning comes from making connections in life, and connections are made by experiencing life. And experiencing life is how we learn. And this is what completes the circle ~ of Life Long Learning.

As Tevye from the movie Fiddler on the Roof says, "L'haim"......To Life!!!! And here is to each of us being able to scratch or fiddle our own way through our journey in life!

~

Chapter Sixteen

Resources You May Wish to Utilize on Your Life Long Learning Journey

Books on Homelearning

- "Natural Learning Rhythms" by Josette and Sambatha Luvmour
- "Carschooling" by Diane Flynn Keith
- "Dumbing Us Down: The Hidden Curriculum of Compulsory Schooling, Vol. 1" by John Taylor Gatto
- "Homeschooling Reflections" by Connie Colton
- "Homeschooling on a Shoestring : A Jam-packed Guide" by Melissa L. Morgan and Judith Waite Allee
- "Homeschooling Our Children Unschooling Ourselves" by Alison McKee
- "Help! I'm Married to a Homeschooling Mom: Showing Dads How to Meet the Needs of Their Homeschooling Wives" by Todd Wilson
- "What Video Games Have to Teach Us About Learning and Literacy" by James Paul Gee
- "Situated Language And Learning: A Critique Of Traditional Schooling" by James Paul Gee
- "The Unschooling Handbook" by Mary Griffith
- "I Learn Better by Teaching Myself" by Agnes Leistico
- "Still Teaching Ourselves" by Agnes Leistico
- "The Book of Learning and Forgetting" by Frank Smith
- "Un-Jobbing: The Adult Liberation Handbook" by Michael Fogler

Books on Homelearning(continued)

- "Fundamentals of Homeschooling: Notes on Successful Family Living" by Ann Lahrson-Fisher
- "Trust the Children" by Anna Kealoha
- "The Teenage Liberation Handbook" by Grace Llewellyn
- "Homeschooling Book of Answers: The 101 Most Important Questions Answered by Homeschooling's Most Respected Voices" by Linda Dobson
- "The Art of Education: Reclaiming Your Family, Community and Self" by Linda Dobson
- "And the Skylark Sings to Me: Adventures in Homeschooling and Community-Based Education" by David Albert
- "Homeschooling and the Voyage of Self-Discovery" by David Albert
- "Teach Your Own: A Hopeful Path for Education" by John Holt (1981) *This book was revised and updated by Patrick Farenga as "Teach Your Own: The John Holt Book of Homeschooling," in 2003*
- "Learning All the Time: How small children begin to read, write, count, and investigate the world, without being taught" by John Holt
- "The Unprocessed Child: Living without School" by Fitzenreiter, Valerie

Children's Books on Homelearning

*Note: These are books about homelearners, homelearning children, or with characters that are homelearners *

- "Skellig" by David Almond
- "Where the Red Fern Grows" by Wilson Rawls
- "The Ear, the Eye, and the Arm" by Nancy Farmer
- "Stargirl" by Jerry Spinelli
- "The Golden Compass" by Philip Pullman
- "Little Women" by Louisa May Alcott

Children's Books *(Continued)*

- "The Pippi Longstocking Series" by Astrid Lindgren
- "Allison's Story: A Book about Homeslearning" by Jon Lurie
- "The Sarah, Plain and Tall Series" by Patricia MacLachlan
- "Touching Spirit Bear" by Ben Mikaelsen
- "The Ruby Slippers School Series" by Stacy Towle Morgan
- "Kensuke's Kingdom" by Michael Morpurgo
- "Brian's Hunt" by Gary Paulsen
- "Kandoo Kangaroo Hops Into Homelearning" by Susan Ratner
- "The Monster of the Month Club Series" by Dian Curtis Regan
- "Olympus: It's Not Just a Game" by Scott W. Somerville
- "Surviving the Applewhites" by Stephanie Tolan
- "A Time to Fly Free" by Stephanie Tolan
- "I am a Homeschooler" by Julie Voetberg
- "Little House in the Big Woods" by Laura Ingalls Wilder
- "Little House on the Prairie" by Laura Ingalls Wilder
- "My Family and Other Animals" by Gerald Durell
- "My Side of the Mountain" by Jean Craighead George

Internet Resources

Note: These websites are accurate as of the publication of this book. These are for reference use only. These web site links are listed as a convenience to you. I am in no way connected to these sites other than to provide them as a resource to you for information. My position is to provide all of the knowledge that I have available to me for your benefit. By publishing these links, I take no responsibility and give no guarantees, warranties, or representations, implied or otherwise, for the content or accuracy of these sites.

http://www.lifelonglearning4all.com

http://www.geocities.com/moonwindstarsky/unschooling.html

http://www.homefires.com/

http://www.unconventionalideas.com/wizard.html

Internet Resources(continued)

http://entertainment.upperdeck.com/yugioh/en/

http://www.carschooling.com/

http://borntoexplore.org/unschool/math.htm

http://sandradodd.com/unschooling

http://www.home-educate.com/unschooling/index.shtml

http://homeschooling.gomilpitas.com/

http://www.besthomeschooling.org/

http://www.americanhomeschoolassociation.org/

http://www.angelfire.com/anime/ananka/aasz.html

http://www.nheld.com/default.htm

http://www.home-education.org.uk/articles.htm

http://www.homeedmag.com/wlcm_HEM.html

http://www.pbs.org/kcts/videogamerevolution/

http://www.wired.com/wired/archive/11.05/view.html?pg=1

http://www.geocities.com/Heartland/Hollow/1093/tvandvideogames.html

http://www.lessontutor.com/kd3.html

http://www.123greetings.com/events/ Everyday is a learning day and a celebration of FUN in Life!!! Click on this link to find out what today is!:) Our favorite voted #1 in our house is Donut Day!!! There is also Frog Jumping Day, Cheese Day, Cuddle up Day, Kiss your car day and more! Find out what day it is today!

http://www.alternative-learning.org/

http://www.creatinglearningcommunities.org/

http://www.downloadlearning.com/downloads/index.html

http://www.unschooling.org/index.htm

http://www.free-ed.net/free-ed/

http://www.gracellewellyn.com/

http://www.holtgws.com/index.html

http://www.homeschoolnewslink.com/index.html

http://www.homeschoolmedia.net/

http://www.homeschoolradioshows.com/

http://www.virtual-bubblewrap.com/popnow-insane.shtml Remember playing with bubble wrap! Now you can online too! This is the funny version the regular one is the next link

http://www.virtual-bubblewrap.com/popnow.shtml On both this page and the one above this you can explore and learn all about the invention of bubble wrap!

http://www.cybercones.com/   Create your own icecream! YUM YUM!

http://www.thecookingschool.com/?id_category=19 fast food recipes you can try at home!

http://www.anagramsite.com/

http://www.foldmoney.com/

http://www.imagespeller.com/

http://www.twinkiesproject.com/

http://www.wheresgeorge.com

http://www.homeschool.com/resources/

http://learninfreedom.org/

http://www.geocities.com/Athens/8259/homemag.html

http://www.homeschoolingreflections.com/

http://www.writebackwards.com/ Write anything backwards!

http://www.digitalfilms.com/

http://www.homeschool.com/

http://homeschooling.about.com/

http://www.homestead.com/peaceandcarrots/collegehowto.html

http://www.homestead.com/peaceandcarrots/Orion.html

http://www.howstuffworks.com/

http://www.hsc.org/

http://www.preservenet.com/theory/Gatto.html

http://www.hsfree.com/

http://www.johntaylorgatto.com/

http://www.kidsdomain.com/down/pc/index.html

Internet Resources(continued)

http://www.leapingfromthebox.com/

http://www.fun-books.com/learningresources.htm

http://www.homeschoolingcompanion.com/index.php

http://www.lacarte.org/learning/

http://www.weirdrichard.com/activity.htm

http://www.lifelearningmagazine.com/read.html

http://www.livefreelearnfree.com/

http://www.liveandlearnconference.org/

http://www.mindwareonline.com/mwstore/index.cfm

http://www.boardgames.com/monopolygames1.html?source=overture

http://www.nationalgeographic.com/geospy/

http://www.smart-estore.com/

http://www.nethomeschool.com/

http://www.addictinggames.com/ (because we all learn so much through video games!) (For more information on learning through video gaming, please check out another awesome Life Long Learning resource within James Paul Gee's book entitled "What Video Games Have to Teach Us About Learning and Literacy! He has an amazing view into the world of gaming and learning!

http://www.teachwithmovies.net/indexes-main.htm

http://www.millsberry.com/complex/arcade.phtml

http://www.nothingbutsoftware.com/

http://www.pbs.org/wgbh/nova/

http://www.scn.org/scws/online.html

http://www.computertrainingschools.com/

http://www.kidconcoctions.com/

http://www.great-ideas.org/directry.htm

http://pbskids.org/go/

http://www.pioneer-arizona.com/

http://www.wideopenwest.com/~bmg/puplinks.html

http://www.pagat.com/patience/nerts.html (Squish card game rules)

http://www.kingtut-treasures.com/hiero.htm

http://selfdirectedlearning.com/

http://www.skylarksings.com/

http://www.hoagiesgifted.org/smart_toys.htm#card

http://www.surfnetkids.com/

http://www.takingchildrenseriously.com/

http://www.businessweek.com/2000/00_22/b3683144.htm

http://www.elite.net/~runner/jennifers/thankyou.htm

http://www.barcodemill.com/

http://www.thecrayonhouse.com/

http://www.vgmuseum.com/

http://www.freechild.org/bell.htm

http://unschoolkidz.beverleypaine.com/links.html

http://unschooler.blog-city.com/

http://www.home-educate.com/unschooling/

http://libaware.economads.com/unschool.php

http://homepage.mac.com/pamsoroosh/iblog/unschooling/index.html

http://www.unschooling.com/

http://www.onlinesciencemall.com/

http://www.uptoten.com/

http://www.vbexplorer.com/VBExplorer/game_tutorials.asp

http://www.wahm.com/

http://www.bbc.co.uk/education/megamaths/tables.html

http://www.fcdsoft.com/

http://www.leasttern.com/workshops/butnotleast/neopets.html

http://www.naturalchild.org/guest/john_gatto.html

http://208.183.128.3/tutorials/gameboard.htm

http://worldatlas.com/aatlas/world.htm

http://www.neopets.com/

Internet Resources(continued)

http://www.cnvc.org/

http://www.mybigfamily.org/kidsgames/meihavbooks.php?keyword=all (Reading list of over 1000+ books and texts to download and read!)

http://www.marshmallowpeeps.com/about/factory_tour.html (Virtual tour of the Peeps Factory to see how they are made)

http://www.e-cookbooks.net/library/?hop=inkwell (E-Cookbooks Library! - Discover The #1 Cookbook and Recipe Site In The World!)

http://www.frugalsimplicity.com

http://www.authormania.com

http://www.dohealthnet.com

http://www.theparenteducator.com

http://www.allthatwomenwant.com/

http://www.magscentral.com/ff/ff55xpb.htm (FREE! Subscription to Family Fun)

http://www.allthatwomenwant.com/whatkidswant.html

http://www.pojo.com/ (Forgot this one too even though I talk of it in the book only because I assumed everyone knew this website!)

http://www.marinij.com/Stories/0,1413,234~26641~2749004,00.html

http://www.a-book-in-time.com/

http://www.familyebiz.com/dvdsalesletter.htm

http://www.howtoteachscience.com/hownottoteachscience.html

http://www.houseofthread.com/ (Crystal is a homelearning friend of mine and she makes some awesome bags and accessories!)

http://www.planetpals.com/ (Another homelearning friend of mine Judith, and AWESOME site!)

http://www.scientificsonline.com/
http://www.pibmug.com/files/map_test.swf

http://www.homeschooloasis.com/article_chart.htm#dts
http://www.philtulga.com/resources.html

http://www.universalpreschool.com/

http://www.homefires.com/clickschool/

http://www.stevespanglerscience.com/

Internet Resources(continued)

http://www.kidzworld.com/site/p4726.htm

http://www.potatoesforschools.org.uk/GYOP/webcam.html

http://www.irishcultureandcustoms.com/1Kids/1Home.html

http://www.mindful-mother-magazine.com/

http://plans.kitez.com/ (all types of kites to make)

http://www.legionkids.org/

http://bensguide.gpo.gov/

http://www.sanford-artedventures.com/

http://artsedge.kennedy-center.org/teach/wlk.cfm

http://alwayslearningbooks.com.au/

http://www.ed.uri.edu/SMART96/ELEMSC/SMARTmachines/machine.html

http://www.bedfordstmartins.com/litlinks/home.htm

http://www.mountvernon.org/virtual/index.cfm/ss/2/

http://curry.edschool.virginia.edu/go/frog/home.html

http://www.5dollarsoftware.com/

http://www.exploratorium.edu/exploring/exploring_chocolate/index.html

http://www.wor.com/shopping/

http://kids.learn2type.com/

http://www.cotf.edu/ete/modules/msese/earthsysflr/rock.html

http://www.funshineexpress.com/C_recipes.htm

http://www.vhea.org/dobson.html

http://www.homeschoolzone.com/main.htm

http://members.cox.net/crandall11/money/

http://www.tomshardware.com/2006/01/09/strip_out_the_fans/page2.html
http://www.computerhistory.org/exhibits/online_exhibitions.html

http://dedge.com/flash/hangman/ (great way to learn spelling through hangman!)

http://www.pbs.org/wgbh/nova/easter/explore/ (all about Easter Island)

Internet Support Groups

Note: These internet support groups are accurate as of the publication of this book. These are for reference use only. These internet support group links are listed as a convenience to you. I am in no way affiliated to these groups other than as a fellow group member and to provide them as a resource to you for information. My position is to provide all of the knowledge that I have available to me for your benefit. By publishing these links, I take no responsibility and give no guarantees, warranties, or representations, implied or otherwise, for the content or accuracy of these sites.

http://www.unschooling.com/discus/messages/board-topics.html

http://groups.yahoo.com/group/0-homeschoolreviews/

http://groups.yahoo.com/group/a_homeschoolers_haven/

http://groups.yahoo.com/group/AHA-Discussion/

http://groups.yahoo.com/group/AHA-HighSchool-College/

http://groups.yahoo.com/group/AlwaysLearning/

http://groups.yahoo.com/group/AlwaysUnschooled/

http://groups.yahoo.com/group/Carschooling/

http://groups.yahoo.com/group/CCL-LLCs/

http://groups.yahoo.com/group/CrunchyUnschoolers/

http://groups.yahoo.com/group/EmpoweredChildhood/

http://groups.yahoo.com/group/FreeThinking-HomeEducators/

http://groups.yahoo.com/group/HEM-FreeResources/

http://groups.yahoo.com/group/HEM-HomeschoolCafe/

http://groups.yahoo.com/group/HEM-NewHomeschoolers/

http://groups.yahoo.com/group/home-schooling/

http://groups.yahoo.com/group/HomefiresJournal/

http://groups.yahoo.com/group/HOLISTIC_LEARNING/

http://groups.yahoo.com/group/Homeschool_For_Me/

http://groups.yahoo.com/group/LearningCommunities/

http://groups.yahoo.com/group/LiveandLearnConference/

http://groups.yahoo.com/group/livefreelearnfree/

http://groups.yahoo.com/group/NoMoreSpanking/

http://groups.yahoo.com/group/ParentingPennys/

Internet Support Groups(continued)

http://groups.yahoo.com/group/Parents_homeschooling_teens/

http://groups.yahoo.com/group/shinewithunschooling/

http://groups.yahoo.com/group/UN-SCHOOL/

http://groups.yahoo.com/group/unschoolersinternational/

http://groups.yahoo.com/group/Unschooling-Spirituality/

http://groups.yahoo.com/group/unschooling2/

http://games.groups.yahoo.com/group/unschooling_gamers/

http://groups.yahoo.com/group/unschoolingbasics/

http://groups.yahoo.com/group/UnschoolingDiscussion/

http://groups.yahoo.com/group/UnschoolingHighlights/

http://groups.yahoo.com/group/unschoolingourselves/

http://groups.yahoo.com/group/UnschoolingStories/

http://groups.msn.com/HomeschoolingMoms2HomeschoolingMoms

http://groups.msn.com/UnschoolingEclecticSchooling

http://groups.msn.com/Unschooling

http://groups.yahoo.com/group/HomeschoolSupport/

http://groups.yahoo.com/group/Homeschooling_SHEs/

http://groups.yahoo.com/group/sitesforlearning/

Single and Working Parent Internet Resources

Note: These websites are accurate as of the publication of this book. These are for reference use only. These web site links are listed as a convenience to you. I am in no way connected to these sites other than to provide them as a resource to you for information. My position is to provide all of the knowledge that I have available to me for your benefit. By publishing these links, I take no responsibility and give no guarantees, warranties, or representations, implied or otherwise, for the content or accuracy of these sites. Some of the websites listed here are from various homelearning options and backgrounds, however, all of the ideas and concepts here can easily be applied to Life Long Learning.

http://www.mjtate.com/

http://homeschooling.gomilpitas.com/articles/061404.htm

Single and Working Parent Internet Resources (continued)

http://www.teach-at-home.com/AskLynn-110102.asp

http://www.hsc.org/chaos/legal/articles/custody.php

http://www.hsc.org/professionals/legalprimer.php

http://members.tripod.com/acorns3/acorns38.html

http://www.families-first.com/homebiz/news/folger2.htm

http://www.homeeducator.com/FamilyTimes/articles/9-2article15.htm

http://www.homeschooloasis.com/art_single_mom_hs.htm

http://www.pineblossomswebpages.com/raggedyjanet/singleparenthomeschooling.shtml

http://www.homeschoolblogger.com/SingleParentsAtHome/15070

http://homeschoolblogger.com/maggieraye/

http://forum.homeschool.com/forum/forum_topics.asp?FID=37 (Single parents homelearning forum discussion group)

http://groups.yahoo.com/group/1Parent_hs/ (Single parent homelearning yahoo group)

http://groups.yahoo.com/group/home_school_single/ (Single parent Homelearning yahoo group)

http://groups.yahoo.com/group/WORKandHOMESCHOOL/ (Working parents and homelearning yahoo group)

http://www.wahm.com/index1.html (HUGE resources for work at home mom's and families)

http://www.wahm.com/boards/Forum3/HTML/000214.html

http://www.wahm.com/forum/ (Working mom's forum group)

http://wahm.sitesell.com/

http://case-studies.sitesell.com/index.html#WAHM (Case studies of successful work at home mom's)

http://wahm-masters.sitesell.com/

http://www.bizymoms.com/startup.html

http://www.en-parent.com/

http://www.drlaura.com/sah/money.html?mode=view&tile=1&id=3450

http://www.hoagiesgifted.org/making_it_work.htm

Single and Working Parent Internet Resources (continued)

http://www.mompreneursonline.com/topbiz.htm

http://www.familyandhome.org/topics/transition_home.htm

http://www.homeedmag.com/HEM/193/mjwork.html

About the Author

Dr. Patti "Diamondlady" Diamond, DD is a life long learning mom - living and discovering life's possibilities along side her husband, Aaron and her three beautiful boys ~ ages 15, 9, and 8. Utilizing her vast amount of experience, knowledge, and research on home learning, Patti has been able to transform her life, her children's lives, and the lives of those around her into what she has termed as Life Long Learning.

In addition to the writing of this book, Patti is also an active member in the homelearning community. She currently is a homelearning parkday group leader. Patti has also been featured in CHN's (California Homeschoolers Network's) California Homeschool News, as part of a two part series on Life Long Learning, Children of the New Earth Magazine, as well as, other freelance articles on the topic.

Patti's vision is to make a difference in people's lives within the homelearning community and beyond - by being a voice of experience and encouragement; by giving back to the community the inspiration and information that she has acquired on the path she has taken, so as to support others in their own journey of discovery.

Patti's ultimate dream is to bring Life Long Learning to people all over the globe - enabling each and every child, each and every family to be free to learn what, when, where and how they wish to learn - free from the constraints of compulsory education - creating the ability for everyone to discover the infinite possibilities that are available through Life Long Learning.

~

Printed in the United States
71843LV00006BA/36